A SHORT HISTORY OF CHILE

Colección
FUERA DE SERIE

A SHORT HISTORY OF CHILE

© 1996, SERGIO VILLALOBOS R.
Inscripción N° 96.666, Santiago de Chile.

ISBN 956-11-1405-4

First Editión, July 1996.
Second Editión, May 1998.
Third Edition, September 1998.
Fourth Edition, March 2000.
Fifth Edition, November 2002.

Edited by John D. Chaburn

PRINTED IN CHILE

SERGIO VILLALOBOS R.

A SHORT
HISTORY OF CHILE

EDITORIAL UNIVERSITARIA

CONTENTS

INTRODUCTION

Interest in the history of Chile has recently reawakened. Scholars are engaged in detailed research, and essayists are proposing interpretations that make the past meaningful. But, above all, it is the anxieties of the present that drive Chileans to seek in their history an explanation of their current problems. What were our people really like? How has this nation been shaped? What is the most precious legacy of our past?

This *Short History of Chile* has no great pretensions. Its purpose is to provide a simple outline containing basic information intelligible to all. No complicated elaboration and no difficult terminology are therefore to be found here, although all the necessary facts are supplied for an understanding of the historical course of our country.

This book, then, offers a small but complete picture that makes it possible to learn, rather painlessly, about the key events in the history of Chile.

THE INDIGENOUS CULTURES

The First Ethnic Groups

The earliest inhabitants of America arrived from Asia in various waves and groups.

Anthropologists who have researched this topic offer different explanations.

The most accepted theory is that Mongol and Eskimo groups crossed the Bering Strait on their way to Alaska. In very remote times, between 10,000 and 40,000 years ago, there were glacial periods during which the ice masses increased in high-latitude areas and high elevation areas. As a result, the level of the sea waters dropped considerably. When the waters fell, a strip of land that united Asia to America surfaced at the Bering Strait.

Groups from Asia could thus cross to America and fan out over the continent.

It is also possible that at the end of the glacial periods other groups might have crossed the Bering Strait in small craft.

Another theory, which supplements the previous one, suggests that America may have been populated by Malay and Polynesian groups that sailed from island to island across the

11

Pacific Ocean. These groups might have landed in various regions, and be the ancestors of Indians with different physical and cultural characteristics.

In our times, successful voyages by explorers on crudely constructed rafts have shown that vast expanses of the ocean can be crossed in primitive craft.

The people who migrated to America were hunters and gatherers whose diet consisted of wild growths and the meat of whatever animals and birds they could kill. Over thousands of years these migrants evolved into the distinct indigenous peoples of the Americas. Some of these peoples, the Aztecs of Mexico, the Mayas of Central America, and the Incas of Peru developed sophisticated civilizations; other groups remained at a primitive cultural level.

THE ANCIENT INHABITANTS OF CHILE

The first inhabitants of Chile came from the north. These bands of hunters and gatherers apparently settled at the foot of the *altiplano andino* (Andean highlands), where rivers and streams

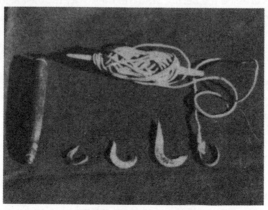

Shell and thorn fishhooks and sinker.

made life possible. In the vicinity of San Pedro de Atacama, archeological remains from 11,000 years ago have been found. Remains just as ancient have been unearthed at Los Vilos and Taguatagua, where at one time there was a lake. Groups also reached the Magallanes region, from Patagonia, and engaged in hunting and fishing.

Some of these groups settled on the northern coast. The humidity permitted the growth of a sparse vegetation, and the availability of fish and shellfish created advantageous living conditions. The hunting of guanacos supplied them with meat.

Coves offered shelter for these groups, and the inhabitants left an unmistakable mark of their residence: huge shell-mounds, several meters deep, the result of long periods of accumulation of shells discarded after meals.

Items found in these kitchen middens include shell and bone fishhooks and a variety of stones coarsely hammered into arrowheads and spearpoints, scrapers, and mortars.

With the passing of time, the shell-mound people engaged in some agricultural tasks, including the cultivation of squash and maize. They also made pottery, which consisted mainly of very coarse vessels.

The Natives at the Arrival of the Spaniards in Chile

DIFFERENT ETHNIC GROUPS

At the time of the arrival of the Spaniards, the natives who populated the present territory of Chile represented a great variety of cultures.

There were groups at a very primitive stage, nomadic bands of hunters and gatherers who moved from place to place in search of food.

Other groups had become farmers, although they had not quite abandoned hunting and gathering. They had settled permanently on the land and engaged in the breeding of llama herds; they also made pottery and textiles. Their houses were built of sturdy materials, and they lived in small, compact villages.

One civilization, that of the Incas, had spread through the north and center of the country and superimposed itself on the other groups. The Incas were part of a huge empire with an excellent material culture and a superior degree of organization.

The most important groups, according to their cultural level, were the *Changos, Chonos, Fueguinos*, and *Pehuenches*.

CHANGOS, CHONOS, FUEGUINOS AND PEHUENCHES

The Changos were the descendants of the shell-mound people, and lived in the coves, and along the shores, of northern and central Chile. Contact with other cultures had enriched their material goods. They manufactured different kinds of pottery vessels, plantfiber baskets, leather goods, and some metal objects.

The ocean, however, continued to be the Changos' main source of sustenance. Using inflated rafts made from sealskins, they were able to harvest the sea.

The Chonos inhabited the islands south of Chiloé, and also lived mainly on seafood. In fragile craft, they traveled around the coasts of the islands.

The Fueguinos, who inhabited the archipelagos south of the Strait of Magellan, were culturally the most primitive. They consisted of three tribes -the *Onas*, the *Yaganes*, and the *Alacalufes*- with more or less similar characteristics.

The Onas lived on the island of Tierra de Fuego and hardly ever ventured into the sea. The Yaganes and the Alacalufes constantly navigated their small canoes through the Magellan channels.

A . Plan d'une Balse faite de peaux de loups marins cousues et pleines d'air
B . Indien sur une Balse vüe de Coté. C . autre vüe de front
D . Traverses pour rassembler les deux moitiez de la balse E troupeau
loupier et la remplir d'air. F. maniere de Coudre les peaux
G . Loup marin a terre H Pingouin

N. Guerard fecit

Chango on a sealskin raft.

The Fueguinos were fishermen and hunters. Their diet included fish, shellfish, seal, and the remains of dead whales washed ashore. Their housing consisted of a small framework of sticks, covered with guanaco hides or sealskins, which they easily assembled and dismantled.

Their scarce clothing consisted of fur skins and hides, although they also bore the hardships of the climate, even the snow, completely naked.

Different were the characteristics of the Pehuenches, a

Chiloé canoe.

nomadic people who inhabited the cordillera opposite the Araucanía. Their bands raided the Patagonian pampa. They hunted the guanaco and covered themselves with its skin, and they lived under shelters made of branches and hides. Their main food was the *pehuén* (pine nut) from the *araucaria* tree; indeed, their name means the pine-nut people. The customs of the Pehuenches were strongly influenced by those of the Araucanians.

THE ARAUCANIANS

The Araucanians lived in the region between the Itata and the Toltén rivers.

Pehuenches.

They were primitive farmers who grew maize and potatoes. They also gathered wild growths and hunted animals and birds. They possessed llama herds and hunted pumas and guanacos.

They used clay and wooden utensils of very rough manufacture. In contrast, their *ponchos* and blankets, woven from llama and guanaco wool, had beautiful colors and designs.

They lived in *rucas*, spacious huts made of wooden poles and branches that protected them from the cold and rain.

Their hunting and fighting implements included bows and arrows, slings, spears, and *macanas* (long, hard sticks with one curved end).

The Araucanians thought that the natural world was animated by spirits. These spirits expressed themselves in the wind, the rain, the crackling of a board, or the fluttering of an insect.

They believed that diseases were caused by evil spells. A *machi*, or witch, was called upon to perform a *machitún*, a kind of magical ceremony that allowed her to discover the cause of

17

Araucanians.

the illness or the person responsible for it. The *machi* would pretend to extract an insect from the patient's body, or she would name a culprit, on whom the patient's relatives would later take vengeance.

The dead, according to the Araucanians, dwelled beyond the sea or the *cordillera*. In the next life they needed the same things as in this life, and for this reason the dead were buried

18

Valdivia pottery.

with their weapons and utensils, food and jars of *chicha*, an alcoholic beverage of fermented grape or apple juice.

Each tribe had a kind of god, el *Pillán*, who represented the spirit of their ancestors. There was also a higher Pillán, a god of good and evil.

Some small groups recognized the authority of the *caciques* (chieftains), and together they formed *rehues* (clans) that had a common ancestor.

There was no central government, but the arrival of the Spaniards led the clans on occasion to join forces to fight against their common enemy. They then elected a *toqui*, and a number of rehues, or all of them, put themselves under his command. Once the campaign was over, the caciques and their men disbanded.

Other peoples, with similar traits, lived in the vicinity of the Araucanians. Immediately to the north were the *Picunches* and, to the south, the *Huilliches*.

ATACAMEÑOS AND DIAGUITAS

The Atacameños and the Diaguitas were peoples who had developed beyond a primitive level of culture.

The Atacameños lived in groups in oases in the Atacama Desert. The group that has been most studied by archeologists is that of San Pedro de Atacama.

The harsh climate, the arid lands, and the scarcity of resources forced the Atacameños to use their intelligence to overcome the hardships of nature.

By means of irrigation canals they carried the scarce waters of the brooks to narrow terraces, spaced at regular intervals on the slopes of ravines, where they grew their crops. They also had herds of llamas, vicuñas, and alpacas.

Diaguita Culture: Duck-shaped jar.
Photograph: Osvaldo Silva G.

Atacameña mummy from San Pedro de Atacama.

Their textiles and clothes were quite remarkable. They made multicolored blankets, shirts, and ponchos and embroidered them with stylized animals and geometric designs.

They were acquainted with the metallurgy of copper and bronze and, to a lesser degree, with that of silver and gold. The beauty of their pottery and baskets was outstanding.

Their houses, very compact in appearance, were built of crudely worked stones; the roofs were made of poles and reeds. The houses were closely grouped in little, stepped villages, full of rugged paths. Some of these villages resembled strongholds, and were called *pucaras* (forts).

The Diaguitas lived further south. They had settled in the valleys between the Copiapó and Choapa rivers.

Snuff inhalation boards of the Atacameños.

Their cultural level was slightly below that of the Atacameños.

The Diaguitas' pottery, very delicate and imaginative, was their most remarkable cultural achievement. Bowls, vessels, plates, and jars featured geometric decorations in white, red, and black. Some vessels imitated human faces, and others the shape of a swimming duck.

Both the Atacameños and Diaguitas were rather few in number.

THE INCA EMPIRE

Seventy years before the arrival of the Spaniards in Chile, the Incas expanded their dominion over our land.

Centered in Cuzco, the empire included the regions of what is now Ecuador, Peru, Bolivia, and the Argentine northwest.

The Incas' social organization relied on strict compliance with obligations to the community. The state, headed by an absolute monarch called Inca, was highly developed. The Incas' cities, houses, and temples reflected an advanced civilization. Their material goods, utensils, and clothing were of excellent quality.

The *Camino del Inca*, a network of paved tracks or simple trails, linked the various regions and facilitated communication. *Tambos*, a sort of primitive inn, were located at regular intervals, and the natives living nearby were required to stock up firewood, water, and food for travelers.

The Inca Tupac Yupanqui started the expansion toward Chile. Advancing slowly and overcoming isolated pockets of resistance, his men reached the Maule River. There, they faced the strong hostility of the Araucanians, and the expansion came to an end.

The influence of the Incas in Chile was not very significant, since it lasted a relatively short time. Moreover, the Incas did not attempt to change the customs of subject peoples. Their benign rule allowed them to use their local languages and to practice their local religions.

The dominated peoples, however, were compelled to collaborate on some work projects and to pay tribute in kind or in precious metals, such as gold. On occasion, some native groups were transferred to distant regions.

The Spaniards landed in Peru at a time of internal strife within the Inca empire. The war ended with the victory of the Inca Atahualpa over his half-brother Huáscar, but it had weakened the empire, a circumstance that favored the Spanish conquest.

DISCOVERY AND CONQUEST

The Spaniards in America

EUROPE'S TRADE PROBLEMS

By the end of the so-called Middle Ages (v-xv centuries), trade between Europe and the Far East was flourishing. Silks and other fine fabrics were imported from India, China, and the Moluccas Islands, as were spices such as cinnamon, cloves, pepper, nutmeg, and other seasonings that the Europeans used to flavor their food.

The trade routes were long and dangerous. They went across the deserts and plateaus of Asia, or the Red Sea and the Indian Ocean. All these routes were controlled by the Arabs or by nomadic tribes. The high risks of this trade demanded high profits.

The situation worsened when the Turks conquered Constantinople and began to harass the traders. The Italian republics of Genoa and Venice, which were links in this chain of trade routes, were the most affected.

At about this time, the kingdoms of Portugal and Spain began to explore the Atlantic and the African coast, in the hope of securing commercial advantages. The nation that could circumnavigate the horn of Africa would be able to trade directly with Asia.

Caravel.

Improvements in shipping facilitated these expeditions. New types of vessel, such as the caravel, with a more complicated set of sails and equipped with a stern rudder, superseded the old ships and made it possible to cross large stretches of the ocean.

At the same time, the invention of the *magnetic needle*, or compass, as well as of other devices, enabled pilots to fix the position of their ships at any point on the seas.

The availability of geographical charts and of experienced navigators who knew the sea currents and winds also fostered the development of shipping.

The explorations initiated by Portugal and Spain in the Atlantic area turned out well.

The Portuguese navigators were successful in reconnoitering the African coast, and discovered the Cape of Good Hope at the southernmost tip of the continent. This accomplishment enabled Vasco de Gama to lead an expedition in search of India, which he reached in 1498.

Spain, on the other hand, pointed its explorations to the west, thanks to the services of Christopher Columbus.

Columbus was a Genoese whose father had made a modest fortune in the manufacture of textiles, among other businesses. The young Columbus had participated in these enterprises and had acquired experience as a seaman and as a ship's captain.

Carried away by his interest in geographical exploration, Columbus designed a plan to reach Asia by sailing across the Atlantic and heading west.

In those days, it was well known that the earth was round and, based on this fact, Columbus prepared his plan. In his view, the world was very small and a short voyage would be sufficient to reach Asia.

Of course, Columbus was mistaken: the distance was three times longer than he had imagined, and a huge continental mass, America, running north to south, stood in the way.

Columbus submitted his project to the Portuguese Crown, but to no avail. He then went to Spain and, after many delays, succeeded in awakening the interest of Queen Isabella.

With her support and that of other notables, Columbus managed to fit out three small caravels, the *Santa María*, the *Pinta*, and the *Niña*. He also secured the aid of two experienced mariners, the brothers Martín Alonso and Vicente Yáñez Pinzón.

Despite the difficult passage and the crew's apprehensions, the voyage was successful.

On October 12, 1492, the explorers sighted land. They had discovered America, though they believed they had reached the Asian islands.

On subsequent trips, Columbus and other navigators reconnoitered the islands and coasts of the *Caribbean Sea*.

At the Convent of La Rábida, Columbus explains his ideas to the monks and other residents of Puerto de Palos.

Ferdinand Magellan (Hernando de Magallanes).

New expeditions covered the Atlantic coasts of South America and enlarged the Europeans' geographical knowledge of the continent. Pedro Alvarez Cabral, a Portuguese explorer, landed in Brazil in 1500, and Juan Díaz de Solís sailed as far as the River Plate, while Amerigo Vespucci went even further south.

All these explorations proved to the Europeans that Columbus had not reached Asia, but another continent, America, which interrupted passage to the East.

A Portuguese mariner, Ferdinand Magellan, who had been in India, formed the idea that in the south of America there had to be a passage to the ocean that lay between America and Asia. Obsessed by this idea, Magellan offered his services to the King of Portugal. Obtaining no response, he approached the Spanish court, where the young king, who was to become Charles V, lent him full support.

Magellan succeeded in forming a company to finance the expedition, which consisted of a small fleet of five fully equipped ships.

The voyage was fraught with difficulties and alarms. Magellan had to spend the winter in a cove in Patagonia, and to mercilessly crush an attempted mutiny by executing several officers and sailors.

The expedition resumed, and on November 1, 1520 Magellan finally discovered the passage he was looking for.

For almost a month, the expedition searched the strait that would later take the name of its discoverer. Finally, it found a way out to a great ocean, which was christened the Pacific, because the waters were unusually calm at that time.

Reduced to only three ships, it sailed toward Asia. Lack of food and sickness made the long voyage an ordeal.

Magellan died fighting the natives of the Philippine Islands. Sebastián Elcano, the new commander, took over and continued the voyage with the only remaining vessel: the *Victoria*. On this ship he crossed the Indian Ocean, sailed around Africa, and finally reached Seville.

In addition to discovering the Strait of Magellan, this expedition was the first to sail around the world.

The voyage had lasted three years. Only 17 of the 265 men who had set out from Spain returned home.

While navigators continued to explore the seas and coasts, various leaders and their daring soldiers invaded the American continent and conquered the territory.

Mexico, the center of the rich Aztec Empire, was conquered by Hernán Cortés. Most remarkable was the heroic resistance of the natives and the great riches Cortés obtained.

Equally remarkable was the conquest of Peru, spearheaded by Francisco Pizarro and Diego de Almagro.

From Panama these leaders organized several expeditions

Francisco Pizarro.

31

Diego de Almagro.

by sea in search of the fabulous empire that, according to the natives of the isthmus, lay farther south.

After several attempts, Pizarro succeeded in finding the Inca Empire, and in a bold move he captured its monarch, the Inca *Atahualpa*.

The capture of the Inca was a great moral victory for the Spaniards, who quickly conquered the empire. Cuzco, the capital, fell to Diego de Almagro.

The huge treasure of gold and silver gathered by Atahualpa as his ransom made the conquerors of Peru extraordinarily wealthy.

The friendship between Pizarro and Almagro, however, had been strained by various incidents. To avert further problems, it was decided that Almagro should continue the conquest toward the south.

The natives of Peru spoke of a region called "Chile", very rich in gold, that would satisfy the ambitions of the Spaniards. This prospect filled Almagro and his men with great expectations.

ALMAGRO DISCOVERS CHILE

Gathering all his new wealth, Almagro fitted out an expedition of more than 400 men. The Inca authorities aided him by providing a large number of native bearers who led the pack llamas that carried food and all kinds of utensils, and supported him along the way.

Almagro left Cuzco and headed for the Bolivian highlands, following one of the Inca roads. He skirted Lake Titicaca on his way south.

To enter Chilean territory, he crossed the cordillera of the Andes, over a pass at 4,200 meters, near the Copiapó valley. His men suffered incredible hardships: cold, snow, and lack of

Leaving Cuzco on the way to Chile, painting by
Pedro Subercaseaux.

The first Mass held in Chile, painting by
Pedro Subercaseaux.

food. Some died, others suffered from frostbite. One man removed his boots and was horrified to see that his toes had fallen off. The native bearers had run away early on and had taken with them the llamas and the supplies. Almagro and his men were left to their fate.

Fortunately, Almagro's column succeeded in crossing the Andes and descended into the Copiapó valley. It was 1536, the year of the discovery of Chile.

Almagro then advanced to the Aconcagua valley, where he set up camp. From there he ordered his officers to reconnoiter the territory.

Since they did not find the riches they expected, the expedition decided to return to Peru, which they knew as a region where gold and silver were plentiful.

On the way back they crossed the deserts of the north,

keeping as close as possible to the shoreline, so as not to have to recross the cordillera.

The expedition had been a disaster, and Almagro's life ended in tragedy. The disputes with Pizarro were settled in an armed combat. The discoverer of Chile lost, and later Pizarro's brothers ordered him to be put to death.

The Conquest of Chile

PEDRO DE VALDIVIA

Three years after Almagro returned to Peru, Pedro de Valdivia, one of the most distinguished officers in Pizarro's army, decided to make another attempt to conquer Chile, despite the region's poor reputation.

Valdivia had been born in a village of La Serena de Extremadura, in Spain. He came from a modest family of *hidalgos*

Pedro de Valdivia, print by Antonio de Herrera.

(soldiers who had attained noble status), who owned an ancestral home and had a coat of arms. When still very young, he enlisted in the army of Charles V and fought in Flanders and Italy, under the command of famous generals. His bravery won him the rank of captain before he had turned twenty-five.

Valdivia returned home and married Doña Marina de Gaete, but he did not stay with her for long. The wonderful news that came from America about the possibilities it offered enterprising and resolute men led him to seek a more promising future there.

He landed first in Venezuela and went on to Peru, where he won the confidence of the Pizarro brothers.

Valdivia was strong-willed and ambitious for power. He aspired to immortalize his name by accomplishing a notable feat. He was therefore not interested in the wealth and well-being attained in Peru: his aim was to conquer a territory of his own and to enjoy the position of a great lord.

THE EXPEDITION

Valdivia faced many difficulties in organizing an expedition. He had very little money with which to buy arms and supplies, and the men were not eager to go to a region that promised hardships rather than riches.

He could not enlist more than ten soldiers. However, he had with him Inés Suárez, a brave and strong-willed woman who constantly supported him.

With this small band and a few native bearers, Valdivia left Cuzco and headed south, along the desert road that Almagro had taken on his return to Peru.

During this journey, the column was joined by some groups of Spaniards who had failed in the Bolivian interior. Once his forces had increased to 150 men, the conquest of Chile became a possibility

The founding of Santiago, oil painting by Pedro Lira.

In the Copiapó valley, Pedro de Valdivia took possession of the country in the name of the King of Spain.

Almost a year after leaving Cuzco, the expedition reached the valley of the Mapocho River, an excellent site from which to stage the conquest.

THE FOUNDING OF SANTIAGO

On February 12, 1541, Valdivia founded the first city in Chile and named it Santiago de la Nueva Extremadura. The chosen site was at the foot of the Santa Lucía hill, which the Indians called Huelén, and between the Mapocho River and one of its branches, which ran along what is now the Alameda Bernardo O'Higgins.

A surveyor laid out the streets and divided each block into four lots, which were assigned to the soldiers. The block in the

Farm belonging to Alonso de Monroy and, later, to Diego García de Cáceres

Paredones o Tambillo del Inca

RIO MAPOCHO

Camino a Valparaiso

Calle Sñta de Asoca

Bartolomé Flores

Cañaveral de Avelino Nuñez

Juan de la Peña

Padre Martin

Francisco de Ibarra

Santo Do mingo

Rodrigo de la Roza

Cañada de San Lazaro

Cañada de San Francisco

Paco Gomez

C. de la Merced

Gaspar de la Barrera

Founding of
SANTIAGO
by Pedro de Valdivia
in 1541

Original lay-out of Santiago, according to Thayer Ojeda.

middle was left free to serve as a parade ground (*Plaza de Armas*). On each side of the plaza, sites were reserved for a church and for the houses of the higher-ranking officers.

The scrivener of the expedition drew up a document in testimony of the foundation ceremony.

Days later, Valdivia created a *Cabildo* (municipal government) and appointed the mayors and councilmen from among the most trustworthy residents.

After the city had been founded, the conquerors divided up the lands and the local Indians, in order to begin to produce what was needed.

Large *chacras* (truck farms) on the outskirts of the city were assigned for the production of food. On land further out, *estancias* (estates) were alloted, mainly for the raising of cattle.

Most important was the distribution of the Indians, the purpose of which was to provide the Spaniards with workers.

Groups of up to thousands of Indians were assigned to the most distinguished Spaniards, who, in exchange for their labor, were to take care of, and protect, them. Since the Indians were entrusted to the Spaniards, the system was called *Encomienda* and the beneficiaries, *encomenderos*.

Harquebusiers in the Arauco War.

With Indian labor, the Spaniards built their houses, worked the land, and, more important still, exploited gold placers.

In the Marga Marga creek, the inner course of what is now the Viña del Mar creek, there were placers that yielded large amounts of gold. Subsequently, sizable amounts of gold were found at Quilacoya, near Concepción, and in other areas.

However, the encomienda system lent itself to infinite abuses and cruelties, and was one of the causes of the disintegration of the Indian communities and the decrease in the Indian population.

RESISTANCE OF THE INDIANS

The early years of Santiago's existence were years of unbelievable hardship. The city was attacked and burnt down by the Indians, and the Spaniards had to endure a lack of food and clothing.

Governor Oñez de Loyola fighting with Cacique Anaganamón.

40

The Spaniards fought unceasingly against the Indians until they subdued them. The natives showed great skill as warriors. They attacked the Spaniards in successive waves in order to overwhelm them. They raised fortifications of logs and chose battlefields that put the Spanish cavalry at the greatest disadvantage. They relied on swamps, small forests, and ravines, to protect their flanks.

However, superiority of arms, and horses, ensured the victory of the Spaniards. Moreover, the Indian population of the central valley was not very large.

EXPANSION OF THE CONQUEST

With some meager and sporadic reinforcements in men and arms, the conquest of Chile was able to expand. La Serena was founded in the north, to facilitate communications with Peru. Later, the cities of Concepción, Imperial, Villarrica, Valdivia, and Angol were founded in the south, as were some forts. These settlements, which were located in the heart of the Araucanian Indian territory, had to be heroically defended. Life was continuous warfare, and the settlers could never enjoy the fruits of peace.

The Spaniards' determination to remain in Araucanía was due to the gold deposits there, whose production made it possible to finance the conquest. Other incentives were the fertility of the land and the large number of Indians who could be assigned to work in the encomiendas.

FIRST ARAUCANIAN REBELLION

Twelve years after the beginning of the conquest the Araucanian Indians, who would not accept the domination of the strangers, rose up in arms in a fearsome rebellion.

Arms used in the Arauco War.

The Araucanian forces were advised and led by Lautaro, a young Indian who had served under Valdivia and gained a thorough knowledge of the invaders' strategy. Lautaro used the tactics that had been used by the Indians of the central region. With great numbers of warriors under his command, he achieved major victories.

Lautaro obtained a decisive triumph when he defeated Valdivia at Tucapel in 1553. Valdivia was captured and met a horrible death at the hands of the Indians.

This victory emboldened the rebels. For several years the Spaniards had to struggle desperately: the city of Concepción was abandoned and even the city of Santiago was threatened.

In the end, Lautaro was betrayed by some of the Indians and died fighting at Mataquito, in a surprise attack by the Spaniards.

THE EXPEDITION OF HURTADO DE MENDOZA

A very young officer was appointed the new governor of Chile. He was García Hurtado de Mendoza, whose family belonged to the highest nobility.

Hurtado de Mendoza rebuilt Concepción and then marched into the Araucanía with the intention of crushing the rebellion. In the course of his expedition he came to the aid of various cities. He founded Osorno and explored as far as the gulf of Reloncaví.

ERCILLA, THE POET WARRIOR

Alonso de Ercilla y Zúñiga, a scion of a family of good ancestry, came to Chile in the expedition led by Hurtado de Mendoza.

During his childhood he had been a page to the prince that was heir to the Spanish Crown and later ruled Spain under the

Alonso de Ercilla.

name of Philip II. Ercilla always had the deepest affection and respect for the monarch.

Dazzled by the news from America and particularly by the incredible resistance of the Araucanians, Ercilla decided to go to Chile.

Together with Hurtado de Mendoza he traveled through Araucanía and fought in many battles. Impressed by the courage of his compatriots and of the Indians, he decided to write an epic poem about the struggle of both peoples.

This was the origin of *La Araucana*, which he began to write on the very battlefields of the war.

Ercilla did not remain in Chile for long. On his return to Spain he continued writing his poem, to which he devoted a considerable portion of his life.

La Araucana was dedicated to Philip II. Ercilla's main purpose was to praise the feats of the Spaniards in the Americas.

At the time, Spain was the most powerful of all nations, with armies covered in glory. But the resistance of the Araucanians had so impressed Ercilla that he also sang of their prowess and praised them as the equal of the Spaniards in battle.

A Indienne du Chily broyant du mays pour en faire de la farine
B Indien en Poncho et Polainas
C Indienne en Choñi et yquella
D Indien jettant le laqs au taureau pour l'arreter

Tasks and clothing of the Indians, from Frezier.

The struggle of the conquerors against the Araucanians continued for a very long time. The Spaniards fought in vain to settle the Araucanians' territory.

Armed clashes occurred every year, and there were some general uprisings. The Spaniards' military system was not well organized: they lacked a standing army, and the struggle was carried on by the settlers, who were required to defend their cities. The Governors could count only on these forces and on soldiers who could be recruited only with difficulty. The supplies of arms and equipment from Peru were also insufficient.

At the end of the sixteenth century the situation was deplorable: The gold placers had dwindled, poverty was widespread, and the Spaniards were demoralized by their inability to subdue the Araucanians. In 1598 a rebellion broke out. It began with the death of Governor Martín García Oñez de Loyola and his troops in the surprise attack at Curalaba.

Heartened by this victory, the caciques gathered their men and set siege to the cities south of the Biobío. The Spaniards put up a heroic resistance, despite hunger and other hardships. Finally, all the defenders -men, women, and children- died or were taken prisoner. Angol, Imperial, Villarrica, Valdivia, and Osorno fell.

The disappearance of these cities marked the end of the Conquest of Chile.

THE COLONIAL PERIOD
(1601-1810)

The State

THE KING AND HIS OFFICIALS

The organization of the Spanish Empire was the responsibility of the king, who held absolute power. His will was the last resort in all matters of government.

By means of royal patent letters the king issued general laws and orders on specific subjects. Under the centralized administration, all matters of importance had to be settled at the royal court.

Since innumerable matters had to be dealt with, the king sought the advice of a very important body, the *Consejo de Indias*, which was in charge of all matters relating to America. Another institution, the *Casa de Contratación*, settled all questions related to trade between Spain and its colonies.

To rule America the king appointed *viceroys* and *governors*, who, as his representatives, also wielded great power.

The governor in Chile was directly responsible to the king, although in the most serious and urgent matters he was subject to the authority of the viceroy of Peru.

Although, the kings of Spain held absolute power, they ruled in a benevolent manner. According to the ideas of the time, the monarch was essentially just and kind, and even though he ruled as he pleased, he had to account to God for his actions. At the end of their term of office, the viceroys, governors, and other high ranking officials had to submit themselves to a trial and refute the accusations that a judge, on behalf of the king, or any private person, had made against them. This procedure was intended to prevent abuses by the authorities, but it was ineffective.

The king's power, although absolute, did not mean that his subjects had no rights and could not defend their interests. Matters concerning America were usually settled after consultation with the governor and the cabildo concerned. The king's subjects were given an opportunity to express their opinions and request the solution they considered appropriate.

On occasion, while they were providing him with additional information to enable him to better resolve the matter, the cabildo or other authorities did not comply with the king's orders.

THE JUDICIARY

This branch of goverment, like all other public functions, derived its authority from the king, and was therefore called the "royal judicature".

All subjects could defend their rights by appealing to the judiciary, which enjoyed special power and prestige.

There were various kinds of judges who passed sentence in the first instance. Their decisions could be appealed to the *Real Audiencia* of Santiago.

The Real Audiencia was the supreme court established in each colony. It consisted of four *oidores* (judges) and was presided over by the governor.

The Real Audiencia.

The oidores were high-ranking magistrates who enjoyed the respect of the public. The Crown tried to ensure that they exercised their functions independently and free from pressures. They were even forbidden to marry or to engage in private businesses in the localities where they performed their duties.

Spaniards and their descendants (the criollos) formed the colony's upper social class. Drawing from the *Peruvian Chronicle* by Guzmán Poma de Ayala, XVI century.

Official of the colonial period.

The Audiencia was responsible for ensuring compliance with the laws and for supervising the other authorities. When a matter of great importance affected the colony, the Audiencia, in concert with the governor, issued *government resolutions*.

The rulings of the Audiencia were issued in the name of the king, and the royal seal was affixed to them.

Very important rulings of the Audiencia could be appealed to the Consejo de Indias, whose decisions were unappealable.

The cabildo was one of the most complex and interesting of colonial institutions. It was composed of two mayors and a number of councilmen, usually six, who were responsible for the municipal administration.

As the organ of municipal government, the cabildo had jurisdiction over the town and its vast outlying territory.

In its decisions, the cabildo was guided by the principle of

Daily life in a Chilean town during the colonial period, drawing by Pedro Subercaseaux.

the *common good*, according to which the interests of individuals and groups were subordinated to what was best for the community.

Since the cabildo was an institution that represented the community, it concerned itself with all matters that might be of interest to or affect it. In the town, it was responsible for the maintenance of streets, gutters, and embankments, refuse disposal and landscaping, as well as for elementary education and public festivities. Within its jurisdiction, it constructed and repaired bridges, regulated the exploitation of forests, and so on.

The cabildo also endeavored to regulate economic activity and prevent abuses: it set the fees that could be charged by artisans and professionals, and it fixed the price of commodities. It also prosecuted residents who hoarded food products in order to artificially raise prices.

The first echelon of the judiciary was also in the hands of the cabildo. Both mayors served as trial judges, mostly concerned with everyday matters. These two officials carried a long rod, the symbol of justice.

There was hardly an issue that affected the community that did not somehow fall within the purview of the cabildo. To be well informed and able to respond promptly to routine problems, the cabildo met with the *procurador* (city prosecutor), who was responsible for submitting to the cabildo any matter that required a decision by it.

The cabildo made representations to the governor and the king by sending reports and petitions in defense of the community it represented.

In times of crisis, a *cabildo abierto* (town meeting) was called. This meeting was attended by the most important residents of the town for the purpose of taking decisions that would then be sent to the higher authorities for final resolution.

Martín García Oñez de Loyola.

The Arauco War

Because of the failure of the war against the Araucanians, it became necessary in the early part of the XVII century to establish a border on the Biobío River. Beyond that border, the Indians would be free, and the Spaniards would not try to enter their territories. The location of the frontier, however, would shift, according to circumstances.

The new strategy was applied by Governor Alonso de Ribera, an experienced soldier who had won considerable prestige in the wars in Flanders.

Ribera also succeeded in having the Crown establish a standing professional army in Chile. To this end, it was necessary each year to allocate a considerable sum, the *real situado*, that was sent from Peru.

These innovations made it possible to establish a fairly large and efficient force to guard the border. The war meant that groups of soldiers made up of adventurers and poor mestizos, determined to make a living as best they could, continued to come to Chile. The mestizos were the best soldiers because they were very tough and were familiar with the terrain where the fighting took place.

The money sent from Peru for the upkeep of the army stimulated the Chilean economy, since it was used to buy food, animals, and all kinds of war supplies.

RAIDS AND COUNTER-RAIDS

The establishment of the border did not end the war. Both sides repeatedly crossed it to make raids.

Detachments of the army would cross into Araucanía to

The Malón (detail), from *Gay's Atlas*.

take Indians prisoner, and sell them later into slavery to estate owners further north. These incursions were called *malocas*. The officials and soldiers made good profits from the sale of Indian slaves, and the interest in capturing Indians largely explains the continuation of the war.

The Indians, for their part, attacked the border outposts to avenge wrongs or to steal cattle and other goods. They called these attacks *malones*.

The struggle continued with skirmishes that erupted every year in the spring and summer. Hostilities ceased in the winter.

PEACE PARLEYS

To appease the Araucanians and to discuss the terms of peace, the Spanish authorities used to hold large meetings with the Indians at sites close to the frontier.

The Governor was accompanied by other authorities and a large contingent of troops. The caciques came with their own men, even from distant locations.

For several days the Governor would talk with the caciques and reach an agreement. The talks were followed by displays of military power by both sides and ended in extended feasts and general rejoicing.

But these parleys did not produce the hoped-for results. Before long, the caciques would break their peace pledges.

THE MISSIONS

Both the Spanish Crown and the Church worked to bring Christianity to the Indians. To that end missions were established in the nearby Araucanian territory. They tried to teach the Indians the principles of Christianity and to exert a civilizing influence. In some places the Indians accepted the mission-

Popular pastimes, according to Famín.

ary Fathers, but the missions' successes were quite modest. The Indians continued to adhere to their customs and beliefs.

THE PACIFICATION OF THE ARAUCANÍA

The violence on the Araucanian border lasted for a hundred years, until the middle of the xvii century.

After that, a kind of peaceful coexistence prevailed, and the two peoples, separated by the Biobío river, had many contacts. A very active trade developed, in which the Spaniards and Chileans supplied the Indians with fabrics, knives, arms and alcohol in exchange for cattle and ponchos.

These contacts also resulted in the birth of children of mixed ancestry, the *mestizos*. Some Spaniards lived among the natives, and there were many settlements of converted and friendly Indians who supplied the forts and, from time to time, took part in forays against other settlements.

The contacts between the Indians and the Spaniards were very strained, and violence exploded in the wake of abuses perpetrated by one side or the other. But there were also long periods without fighting.

Life on the frontier was not defined as much by heroism as by a lax routine in which all kinds of abuses and interests were interlaced. The troops led an idle and disorderly life, and their officers engaged in shady deals. All kinds of adventurers thronged the military outposts, missions, and Indian settlements.

The Indians, for their part, would go to the forts and ranches to steal or to scrounge.

Although the war had faded, various interests strove to magnify its importance and to create an image of a fierce struggle: a standing army enabled many people to make a living, the distribution of merchandise bought with the *real situado* lent itself to dishonest transactions that benefited the officers and, on occasion, the governors; and the ranchers wanted to continue to provision the army.

Economy and Society

THE TRADE MONOPOLY

The Spanish Empire, like all colonial empires, was based on the economic dependence of its dominions on the mother country.

The colonies could only trade with Spain. All other nations were totally excluded.

Compliance with this policy was enforced by means of a centralized and controlled commercial system.

The institution responsible for regulating and controlling trade was the *Casa de Contratación*, as was stated earlier.

To transport goods to America, Spain equipped *fleets* and *galleons* every year. One fleet went to Mexico, and the other to Panama. The latter carried the cargo intended for South America.

Traders from Peru would sail in their own ships to Panama, where they bought the goods they needed from the Spanish merchants. Part of the cargo was sent to Chile in exchange for local products. Peru was thus the intermediary for Chilean trade.

Trade was based on the following exchanges:

From Chile to Peru

Hides, tallow, charqui (jerked beef). Wheat, timber, wine, and dried fruits. Gold and silver.

From Peru to Chile

Fine fabrics, china, furniture, paper, iron, arms, and all kinds of European manufactured products. Sugar, cacao, and tobacco.

The Chilean economy was based on crop farming and stock raising. The amount of land available and the forced labor of the Indians from the encomiendas made agricultural production easy and inexpensive.

During the early years, agriculture was little developed because the population was very small. But with the passage of time and the need to supply Peru with wheat, grain exports became very important.

The livestock brought by the Spaniards -cattle, sheep, and horses- increased enormously.

Leather was used for footwear, saddles and bridles, bags, and many other things. Tallow was used for making candles and soap. Charqui was consumed by the less affluent population. Sheep wool was used for blankets, ponchos, and rough fabrics.

The haciendas were the scene of country life and activities. These large estates were worked by the Indians and mestizos. The great fertility of the soil and the limited demand for foodstuffs made intensive farming unnecesary. The soil was only superficially ploughed; the ditches irrigated small plots of land; and no fertilizer was used.

Cattle were raised on open range. The animals roamed the hills and streams, which made it necessary once a year to organize a round-up and to drive them to the hacienda's corrals. The fiesta of the rodeo originated in this activity.

THE ARISTOCRACY

In the wake of the Spanish conquest, a powerful and wealthy aristocracy began to emerge in Chile.

The conquerors and their descendants had taken all the land, and had been alloted the encomiendas which provided

A tertulia (social gathering) in 1790.

labor for the *gold placers* and for farming. They were thus able to accumulate wealth, which they bequeathed to their heirs.

In the xvii century, new families with ties to commerce, public service, and the military emerged and joined the aristocracy.

The *Spaniards* predominated in the early years, but later the *criollos*, their descendants, became important: land, houses, and encomiendas passed into their hands. The Spaniards remained more closely connected with government and commerce.

The aristocracy also enjoyed a high level of culture and was linked to the Church and the Army.

In Chilean society, which was marked by profound social differences and a rigorous hierarchy, the aristocracy exercised an absolute influence over the other sectors.

Its representative organ was the cabildo. Its members came from the aristocracy, and expressed and defended its interests.

In the aftermath of Spanish domination, the Indian population began sharply to decline.

There were various causes for this decline: Diseases brought by the conquerors ravaged the Indian population. Both the *hard labor* imposed by the Spaniards and the abuse of *wine* and *spirits* shortened the lifespan of the Indians. War and the disintegration of Indian families and communities were also responsible for the decrease.

Only the free Indians, who lived south of the Biobío river, maintained their numbers.

North of the river, the Indians had to live alongside their conquerors and abide by their rules. They soon acquired the basic elements of the conqueror's culture, including the *Spanish language* and the Catholic religion. They also adopted the clothing, foods, and other material goods of the Spaniards.

Some groups preserved their lands and villages, but with the passing of time they, too, were dispossessed.

Chilean peasants, from Famin.

The Crown and the Church made great efforts to protect the Indians from the abuses of the encomenderos. To that end a large number of royal warrants were issued, and many priests and authorities conducted campaigns on their behalf. The King even established the office of *Protector de naturales* (Protector of the Natives), whose principal duty was to enforce the protection laws.

Nevertheless, all these measures were in vain. As the Indian population decreased, the number of mestizos increased. The mestizos were the offspring of the Spanards and Indian women. Racial mixing started with the Conquest when the conquerers established unions with Indian women and later with their descendants. The number of mestizo children continued to increase.

The mestizos lived mainly in the countryside: they were peons (laborers) on the haciendas and also worked in the mines. But the low level of productive activities offered them few opportunities. Thus most mestizos lived in great poverty, and idleness and vice characterized their mode of living.

Chile also imported *negro slaves* from Africa, although the slave trade was not as important as in the other colonies.

The price of these slaves was very high, and their transport was long and fraught with danger. Moreover, there were enough Indians and mestizos to provide all the labor needed at the time.

The negro slaves usually worked as domestics or as trusted foremen, and were therefore treated kindly.

Culture

EDUCATION

Elementary education was instituted from the time of the Conquest.

Convents and some private teachers opened schools, but they had a rather precarious existence. Religious orders were also responsible for setting up secondary schools. The most famous was the *Convictorio de San Francisco Javier*, which was run by the Jesuits. When they were expelled from the dominions of the king of Spain in the XVIII century, the Crown financed the establishment of the *Convictorio Carolino*.

Advanced studies were those that prepared students for the priesthood. Both Dominican and Jesuit Fathers successfully established faculties of theology at the so-called *Universidades Pontificias* (pontifical universities) in their convents in the capital.

The Church played a very important role in the culture of the times: education was in its hands, and the priests were the most cultivated persons.

This situation changed in the XVIII century, with the establishment of the *Real Universidad de San Felipe*, which offered a higher education to young men who did not intend to go into the priesthood. The most prestigious fields of study were Theology and Law, and the university conferred the highest academic degree, the doctorate.

Although the programs of study at the Universidad de San Felipe were not very innovative, the university nurtured a generation of brilliant intellectuals, who later participated in the Independence of Chile.

Of great intellectual concern was the writing of chronicles that would leave a historical record of the most important events and facts.

The Spanish conquest and the Arauco war were the events most frequently described by the chroniclers. Indeed, *La Araucana* can be considered a chronicle in verse.

The chroniclers were army officers or priests. They not only told the story of the past but also related the events of their time. The following were four of the most important chroniclers:

Francisco Núñez de Pineda y Bascuñán, a criollo born in Chillán, wrote *Cautiverio Feliz* (Happy Captivity), an account of his life among the Araucanians who captured him in battle. This work is a valuable source of detailed information about the customs of the Araucanians.

Alonso de Ovalle, a Jesuit priest born in Santiago, wrote the *Histórica Relación del Reino de Chile*, a work remarkable for its style and the correctnes of its language, which has made him an authority on the language, as recognized by the Real Academia Española de la Lengua. Ovalle's work is also notable for the affection with which he described the character of Chile: its landscape, its products, and its people.

Diego de Rosales was a Spanish Jesuit who lived in Chile for many years. He worked as a missionary and held high offices in his order. His *Historia General del Reino de Chile* is valuable as a chronicle of the Arauco war and for its description of the Indians and their culture.

In the xviii th century was the abbot Juan Ignacio Molina, a noteworthy Chilean Jesuit who was exiled with the other members of his order. He lived in Bologna, Italy, for most of his life. His two most important works, the *Historia Civil de Chile* and the *Historia Natural de Chile*, were widely circulated and translated into several languages. His second book is not a chronicle but a scientific study of the flora and fauna of the country.

Art was not very important in Chile. There were no creators of great originality in music, painting, or sculpture. Indeed, most works of art were imported from Spain or Peru and reflected European artistic trends.

Artistic activities were closely linked to religion. In painting and sculpture, the subject matter and the persons represented were generally inspired by passages from the Bible or were saints. The wooden polychrome sculptures, often small in size, were usually quite beautiful.

A considerable number of paintings came from Cuzco and Quito, where there were prestigious ateliers. A series of paint-

XVIII art: The child Francis giving food to the poor (detail), Museo Colonial de San Francisco.

ings on the life of Saint Francis of Assisi is preserved in the Franciscan convent in Santiago. The most notable were made by Juan Zapaca Inca, an esteemed Peruvian painter.

The aesthetic of the Renaissance, which sought perfection of form and balance, later gave way to the baroque, a style characterized by contorted and angular figures and an incredible profusion of ornamentation.

In America, the baroque style was infused by Indian taste and thus became a mestizo art. The extant altars and *retablos* in this style are remarkable for their luxuriant and delicate decoration.

During the final decades of the colonial period, the European neoclassical revival, with its return to the aesthetic ideals of the Renaissance -purity of line, simplicity, and harmonious proportions- made its appearance in Chile.

The best example of the neoclassical style in Chile is the *Palacio de La Moneda*, built by the Italian architect Joaquín Toesca. Imposing in its dimensions, the building represents the essence of simplicity and good taste.

The End of the Colonial Period

THE SPIRIT OF THE XVIII CENTURY

The last hundred years or so of the colonial period up to 1810 was a period of slow maturation in Chile and the other dominions of Spain.

In Chile, the population grew at a moderate pace to some 800,000 inhabitants. Commerce expanded, agricultural production increased, and mining again became important. The educational and cultural level also rose.

Within Chilean society, the aristocracy increased its wealth and influence, and refined its culture.

Chilean women, from the *Album de mujeres chilenas*.

In addition, the Arauco war died down. With the exception of two general rebellions, the relations of the Indians with the Spaniards and the Chileans, were characteristically peaceful.

All these changes lent a different semblance to the XVIIIth century that heralds the future independence of the country.

TRANSFORMATION OF THE ECONOMY

The decline of Spanish industry and of its merchant fleet and navy forced the Crown to make changes in its trade system. At the same time, strong pressure was being exerted by England, France, and later the United States, to be allowed to trade with the Spanish colonies.

Chilean house, drawing by Earle.

To boost trade within the empire, the fleets and galleons were eliminated, and individual ships were allowed to ply between Spain and each of the colonies. For the first time Chile could trade directly with Spain in vessels of the *registro del Cabo de Hornos* (named after the route they followed).

Several taxes on commerce were also reduced or abolished. As a result, imports soared and prices dropped.

Finally, the Crown granted special permits for trade with foreign countries, which meant the virtual disappearance of Spain's monopoly of colonial trade.

The trade boom stimulated the Chilean mining industry, because imported manufactures had to be paid for in gold and silver. Many poor mestizo prospectors searched for mineral deposits, and were grubstaked by small businessmen. The districts of the north were the mining centers and produced gold, silver, and smaller amounts of copper.

Cuesta Lo Prado y Rincón de Valparaíso, drawing by María Graham.

The increase in agricultural and mining activities created new public and private wealth, which was reflected in public works, the founding of new institutions, housing construction, and the spending of the aristocracy.

GOVERNMENT AND REFORM

During the xviii th century the Spanish monarchs and their ministers pursued reform policies that had a considerable impact on the mother country and the entire empire. The main purpose of these measures was to revive the Spanish economy by encouraging agriculture, industry, and trade. The finances of the Crown and the structure of the state were also reformed. These policies had profound consequences in America, where they were implemented by the viceroys and the governors.

There was a general spirit of innovation, and it was often the criollos of the aristocracy who proposed or carried out the reforms.

The Cal y Canto Bridge, by John Searle, 1834.

Important changes were made in the following areas:
   a) *The founding of cities.* In many parts of Chile population centers had developed as a result of agricultural and mining

The port of Valparaíso, drawing by Auguste Borget, 1860.

activities. Some governors decided to concentrate these people in cities, so that they could lead orderly lives, under the supervision of the authorities.

Two governors excelled in this endeavor: Domingo Ortiz de Rosas, Count of Poblaciones, and José Manuel de Velasco, Count of Superunda.

The cities of Copiapó, Vallenar, Illapel and San José de

Ambrosio O'Higgins, Baron of Ballenary and Marquis of Osorno.

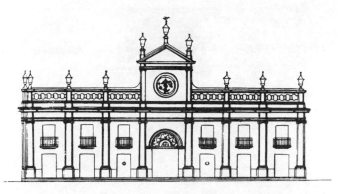

The Tribunal del Consulado.

Maipo were created out of mining centers, while those of Quillota, San Felipe, Rancagua, San Fernando, Curicó, Cauquenes, and Linares became the hubs of large farming areas. Road transport was also responsible for the development of these cities, as well as of Los Andes and Melipilla.

b) *Public Works and Buildings*. The new prosperity made it possible to undertake important public works. Ambrosio O'Higgins, the most notable of the governors and later the viceroy of Peru, showed the greatest concern for public works.

The road from Santiago to Valparaiso, which crossed the ranges of hills at the passes of Lo Prado and Zapata, was built to improve the flow of goods and travelers.

In Santiago embankments were built on the Mapocho river to prevent flooding, and the Cal y Canto Bridge was erected to link the center to the northern district of the city.

Among the buildings, mention must be made of *La Moneda*, a work of vast proportions that entailed huge outlays. In it the mint was installed.

The Cathedral and the church of Santo Domingo also date from this period. Like La Moneda the Cathedral was designed by the Italian architect Toesca.

Para el dia 18. del corriente
à las 9. de la mañana: espera
à V. el M. I. S. Presidente,
con el Ilustre Ayuntamien-
to, en las Salas del Real
Tribunal del Consulado, à
consultar y decidir los medios, mas oportunos à la de-
fensa del Reino y publica
tranquilidad.

The cabildo of 1810 (invitation card).

74

c) *New institutions*. In line with the ongoing changes in the country, the state had to adapt its organization or create new institutions.

The already mentioned *Universidad de San Felipe* responded to the need to provide a complete program of higher studies for young Chileans.

The *Casa de Moneda* was established to mint the gold and silver mined in Chile. This money was required to make up for the lack of currency with which to pay for imports.

The *Tribunal del Consulado* was established for the purpose of dealing promptly with commercial cases.

To better handle local matters, two *intendencias* (administrative units) were set up, one in Santiago, the other in Concepción.

THE ENLIGHTENMENT

The Enlightenment is the name given to the doctrine of the philosophical movement embraced by the most cultivated elite of the European continent in the xviii th century. Its core ideas were eminently critical: reason was to be used to question everything -customs, religion, the monarchy, colonialism.

Society and its mores were the target of ironic criticism by Voltaire in his *Essai sur les moeurs*. He was also a declared enemy of the Church.

In political philosophy, the most outstanding works were Montesquieu's *L'esprit des lois* and Jean Jacques Rousseau's *Contrat Social*. In these analyses of political systems, these two authors laid the ideological foundations of republicanism, democracy, and representative government.

These works and others like them were the intellectual underpinnings of the Enlightenment.

The Enlightenment reached America and Chile through various channels. Some books managed to enter the country despite the prohibitions imposed by the Crown. A number of criollos had become acquainted with the new ideas during their trips to Spain or other countries, and they subsequently passed on what they had learned. The activities and reforms of the governors also helped to create a new spirit.

Two criollos were noteworthy for their "enlightened" ideas: José Antonio de Rojas and Manuel de Salas.

Rojas brought into the country a variety of European works, such as the *Encyclopédie* compiled by Diderot and D'Alambert, a critical summary of the knowledge of the times. He also introduced the *Essai philosophique sur les établissements*

Manuel de Salas, engraving by N. Desmadryl.

européens by the Abbé Reynal, a fierce criticism of the colonial policies of the European nations, including Spain.

Manuel de Salas distinguished himself by his innovative spirit and by his many endeavors to serve his people. Most important were his ideas and efforts to find new sources of economic wealth and to foster agricultural, mining, and handicraft production. His work and his reports to the Tribunal del Consulado opened up new possibilities, but his most significant achievement was the establishment of the *Academia de San Luis*. There, he introduced programs of technical studies to enable youths to earn a living in productive employment.

All these innovations show that a new spirit had reached the country.

WORLDWIDE POLITICAL CHANGE

The final decades of the XVIII th century saw several momentous events that had worldwide consequences and affected the Spanish colonies.

The first was the *Declaration of Independence of the United States* (1776). In freeing themselves from British domination, the colonies of North America showed other colonies that, with will and determination, they could achieve independence and, furthermore, that it was possible to establish a republican goverment and to administer a nation by means of a constitution that limited the power of the authorities and protected the rights of the people.

The second important event was the *French Revolution*, which began in 1789. The French monarchy was overthrown and put to death at the guillotine. The people took power under the slogan of Liberty, Fraternity, Equality, and their leaders initiated a profound reform of the existing order. However, instead of achieving its proclaimed ideals, the revolution led to bloodshed and anarchy.

These two events were a manifestation of the ideas that were sweeping Europe and America.

THE ARISTOCRACY AND THE ETHOS OF THE CRIOLLOS

By the end of the colonial period, the criollo aristocracy had become an extremely important group. The development of agriculture, mining, and commerce had increased its wealth and power.

Wealthy and upperclass families had established the *mayorazgo*, the right of the eldest son to inherit the most valuable share of a family's properties and goods. The aristocracy had also acquired titles of nobility, which further highlighted their social status. Education, reading, and travel had expanded their cultural horizons. They also had a strong awareness of their own worth and felt called upon to play a decisive role in the life of the colony.

The aristocracy confused their aspirations with the interests of the country, which they loved as something they owned.

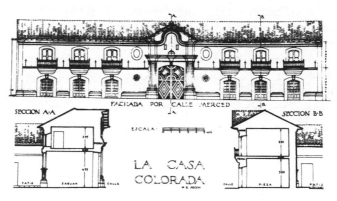

The Casa Colorada, drawing by Eduardo Secchi,
Architecture in Santiago, 1941.

This love of their native soil was deeply rooted in the criollos. They loved all things typical of Chile and its countryside and they had high hopes for the future of their country. The fertility of the land, the abundance of minerals, the mildness of the climate, and the riches of the sea nourished their illusions and led them to conceive a great and prosperous destiny for Chile.

They did not realize that those dreams could only come true over the course of many years.

DISCONTENT AND REFORMIST IDEAS

The new ideas and the criollos' aspirations for reform collided with colonial reality, and this collison fostered a growing discontent.

The three mayor areas of dispute were as follows:

a) *Economic policy.* The criollos wanted to limit foreign trade because excessive imports had ruined many local businesses by driving prices down. Moreover, they thought that the outflow of gold and silver was impoverishing the country, and blamed the competition of foreign products with domestic goods for the decline of local crafts.

They also wanted to find new sources of wealth, to increase production, and to process raw materials; all of which they hoped would bring prosperity to the colony.

Finally, they complained about taxes, which they deemed excessive.

b) *Culture.* The best educated Chileans thought that the Spanish state was not sufficiently concerned about education and that instruction was too old-fashioned. It was therefore the criollos themselves who tried to innovate. They founded the Universidad de San Felipe and the Academia San Luis, but they were unable to fully achieve what they wanted in this area.

There were also complaints about the banning of books the Crown and the Church considered dangerous, especially those printed abroad. However, the desire to have a printing press in the country was never fulfilled.

c) *Politics*. From early times the criollos complained that their merits went unrecognized and that they were passed over in appointments to public office, even though many of them held government positions. Nonetheless, the highest positions, including that of governor, were always given to Spaniards.

This system prevented the criollos from participating directly in the government of their country. Furthermore, all decisions of importance were made at the Spanish Court.

All these circumstances contributed to the frustration of the criollo aristocrats, who believed that the destiny of their native land belonged to them.

INDEPENDENCE
(1810-1823)

La Patria Vieja (The Old Fatherland)

THE INVASION OF SPAIN

In 1808 Napoleon invaded Spain as part of his plan to dominate Europe. King Ferdinand VII and the royal family were taken to France as prisoners, and the French emperor put his brother, Joseph Bonaparte, on the Spanish throne.

The Spanish people immediately reacted and prepared themselves to face the invader.

In the absence of a legitimate king, the *Junta Central*, composed of distinguished notables, was established to rule Spain on behalf of the monarch.

THE POLITICAL IDEAS OF THE CRIOLLOS

In Chile, as in all the Spanish colonies in America, the criollos were *sincerely and absolutely loyal to the king*. The Spanish king was respected and venerated as the head of the empire, within which the kingdom of Chile found its *raison d'être* and historical identity.

Thus the imprisonment of Ferdinand VII provoked outrage and, like the Spanish people, the Chileans prepared themselves to defend the rights of their king.

Their affection for the king, however, did not mean that there were no complaints against his rule: as we have already seen, there were good grounds for their discontent and they wished to institute a number of reforms. But despite their aspirations, the criollos did not intend to break with Spain; on the contrary, they looked to the king and his agents to solve their problems.

In any event, the criollo aristocracy wanted to have more of a say in the government.

Only an *insignificant minority* thought about independence, and they hardly dared express their ideas.

THE FIRST JUNTA

While the French invaders were trying to consolidate their position in Spain, the Chilean criollos decided to form a junta, similar to the one in Spain, that would rule on behalf of the king while he was in prison.

In this way, they hoped to *preserve the sovereignty of Ferdinand VII* while participating in the government of the country and carrying out the reforms they wanted. In sum, the junta embodied both the weight of tradition and the aspirations for change.

The criollos succeeded in persuading the interim governor, Mateo de Toro y Zambrano, Conde de la Conquista and a native Chilean, to convene an open cabildo on September 18, 1810.

The most prominent residents of Santiago, almost all of whom had been born in Chile, met with the cabildo and the authorities in the Tribunal del Consulado building.

On opening the meeting, Toro Zambrano announced that he wished to relinquish his office, and placed his baton of

First National Congress.

command at the disposal of the assembly. Attorney General José Miguel Infante then proposed that a government junta be formed to preserve the kingdom for the monarch, and he explained the reasons that justified this action.

The motion was unanimously approved, and the following persons were elected:

President: Mateo de Toro y Zambrano.

Vice-President: Bishop José Antonio Martínez de Aldunate.

Members: Juan Martínez de Rozas, Juan Enrique Rosales, Ignacio de la Carrera, Fernando Márquez de la Plata, and Francisco Javier de Reina.

Secretaries: Gregorio Argomedo and Gaspar Marín

Mateo de Toro y Zambrano.

At this same meeting, the members of the junta took their oaths of office and the junta was officially established.

PRINCIPAL MEASURES AND REFORMS

a)   *Defense.* To protect the country from foreign attack, new infantry and cavalry forces were established and the militia reorganized.

b)   *Freedom of trade.* Although the idea of further expanding trade was absolutely resisted, the junta decided to adopt a freer trade policy. The idea was unpopular with the people at large and with businessmen, who opposed it through the Tribunal del Consulado.

The junta's trade policy was motivated by the need to maximize customs revenue. Only if this were done could the junta meet urgent defense expenditures, buy arms from abroad, and finance the reforms it had in mind.

Under a decree issued in 1811, the ports of Coquimbo, Valparaíso, Talcahuano, and Valdivia were declared open to trade with friendly and neutral nations.

This measure complemented the commercial reforms made earlier by the Crown.

c) *Establishment of a Congress*. This was the most far-reaching reform implemented by the junta, since it entailed the recognition of the *people's sovereignty* and the formation of a *representative government*: the nation had the right to rule itself and to elect its officials.

In essence, this measure contradicted the absolute power of the king.

The congressional deputies were elected by the most prominent residents at meetings held in each city.

FIRST NATIONAL CONGRESS

On July 4, 1811, the Congress was installed during an imposing ceremony. Juan Antonio Ovalle was elected president.

Within Congress, two currents of opinion soon surfaced. One group was led by Dr. Juan Martínez de Rozas, long an influential voice, and included Bernardo O'Higgins. This group harbored a deep desire for major reforms, and some of its members secretly promoted the idea of independence, as did O'Higgins.

The second, and far larger, group better reflected the prevalent mood in Chile. They wanted to carry out only moderate reforms, and some were staunch royalists.

The main measures taken by Congress included:

a) *Reform of the judiciary*. To replace the Real Audiencia, a Tribunal de Apelaciones was set up, and a Tribunal Supremo Judiciario was established to put an end to the filing in Spain of appeals to the Consejo de Indias.

These measures ensured that the administration of justice was located in Chile and that all judges were Chilean.

b) *Abolition of slavery*. Chile became the third country in the world to take this humanitarian step.

85

A decree issued in 1811 prohibited the import of slaves and declared that the children of slave women would be born free. These provisions did not immediately eliminate slavery, which was destined inevitably to disappear as time went on.

CARRERA'S GOVERNMENT

Meanwhile, rivalries had arisen among the criollos. The clash of currents of opinion and the rivalries between family groups led to José Miguel Carrera becoming president of a new junta.

Carrera belonged to one of the most aristocratic families in Chile. His father, Ignacio de la Carrera, had been a member of

José Miguel Carrera.

NOCIONES FUNDAMENTALES SOBRE LOS DERECHOS DE LOS PUEBLOS.

TODOS los hombres nacen con un principio de sociabilidad, que tarde ó temprano se desembuelve. La debilidad, y larga duracion de su infancia, la perfectibilidad de su espíritu, el amór maternal, el agradecimiento y la ternura, que de él nacen, la facultad de la palabra, los acontecimientos naturales, que pueden acercar, y reunir de mil modos à los hombres errantes y libres: todo prueba que el hombre está destinado por la naturaleza á la sociedad.

El fuera infeliz en este nuevo estado, si viviese sin reglas; sin sujecion, y sin leyes, que conservasen el órden. ¿Pero quien podia dar, y establecer estas leyes, quando todos eran iguales? Sin duda el cuerpo de los asociados, que formaban un pacto entre si de sujetarse á ciertas reglas establecidas por ellos mismos para conservar la tranquilidad interior, y la permanencia del nuevo cuerpo, que formaban. Asi pues el instinto, y la necesidad, que los conducia al estado social, debia dirigir necesariamente todas las leyes morales, y politicas al resultado del órden, de la seguridad, y de una existencia mas larga y mas feliz para cada uno de los individuos, y para todo el cuerpo social. Todos los hombres, decia Aristoteles, inclinados por su naturaleza á desear su comodidad, solicitaron, en conseqüencia de esta inclinacion, una situacion nueba, en fluebo estado de esas cosas, pudiese procurarles los mayores bienes posibles: tal fué el origen de la sociedad.

El órden y libertad no pueden conservarse sin un govierno; y por esto la misma esperanza de vivir tranquilos, y dichosos, protegidos de la violencia en lo interior, y por los insultos hostiles, compelió á los hombres ya reunidos á depender, por un consentimiento libre, de una autoridad pública. En virtud de este consentimiento se erigió la *Potestad Suprema*, y su exercicio se confió à uno, ò à muchos individuos del mismo cuerpo social.

En este gran cuerpo hai siempre una fuerza central, constituida por la voluntad de la nacion para conservar la seguridad, la felicidad, y la conservacion de todos, y prevenir los grandes inconvenientes que nacerian de las pasiones: y se observa tambien una fuerza centrifuga, que proviene de los esfuerzos, injusticias, y violencias de los pueblos vecinos, por las quales obran unos sobre otros para extenderse, y agrandarse à costa del mas debil; à menos que cada uno se haga respetar por la fuerza. Por este principio la historia nos presenta à cada paso la esclabitud, los estragos, la atrocidad, la miseria, y el exterminio de la espesie humana. De aqui es que no se encuentra algun pueblo, que no haya sufrido la tirania, la violencia de otro mas fuerte.

Este estado de los pueblos es el origen de la monarquia, por que en la guerra necesitaron de un caudillo, que los conduxese à la victoria. En los antiguos tiempos, dice Aristoteles, el valor, la pericia, y la felicidad en los combates elevaron à los capitanes, por el reconosimiento, y utilidad pública, à la potestad real.

No tuvo otro origen la monarquia española. Los Reyes Godos ¿que fueron en su principio sino Capitanes de un pueblo conquistador? ¿Y de qué le huviera servido al Infante Don Pelayo decender de los Reyes Godos, si los españoles no huviesen conocido en él los talentos, y virtudes necesarias para restaurar la nacion, y reconquitar su libertad?

Establescamos pues como un principio, que la autoridad suprema trahe su origen del libre consentimiento de los pueblos, que podémos llamar pacto, ò alianza social.

En todo pacto intervienen condiciones, y las del pacto social no se distinguen de los fines de la asociacion.

Los contratantes son el pueblo, y la autoridad executiva. En la monarquia son el pueblo, y el rey.

El rey se obliga à garantir y conservar la seguridad, la propiedad, la libertad, y el órden. En esta garantia se comprehenden todos los deberes del monarca.

El pueblo se obliga à la obediencia, y á proporcionar al rey todos los medios necesarios para defenderlo, y conservar el órden interior. Este es el principio de los deberes del pueblo.

El pacto social exige por su naturaleza que se determine el modo con que se hade exercerse la autoridad pública: en que casos, y en que tiempos se hade oir al pueblo; quando se le hade dar cuenta de las the first junta; his brothers Juan José, Luis, and Javiera were his most loyal supporters. He had begun his military career in Spain, but on hearing news of the events in Chile he had returned home, eager to take an active part in them.

By force of arms, he had himself made head of the government and then proceeded to dissolve Congress.

Carrera's government pursued a bold policy that was destined to pave the way for independence. The most important measures it took included:

a) *La Aurora de Chile*. At about that time a printing press was brought to Chile by a North American citizen, Matthew Arnold Hoevel. The government bought it, put Fray Camilo Henríquez in charge of it, and ordered him to publish a newspaper. From the first issue, the newspaper *La Aurora de Chile* began to spread new ideas based on those of the philosophers of the Enlightenment, particularly Rousseau. Carried away by his enthusiasm, Camilo Henríquez went so far as to openly suggest that it was necessary for Chile to proclaim its independence.

Plaza de Armas, from *Gay's Atlas*.

Fray Camilo Henríquez, publisher of La Aurora de Chile.

b) *National symbols*. To indicate that Chile was a different entity from Spain, a national flag was designed, having three horizontal bands -blue, white, and yellow- as was a similarly colored cockade.

c) *Provisional Constitution of 1812*. One of the most important political aspirations of the patriots was the drafting of a constitution that would enshrine the rights of the people and regulate the power of the authorities.

A group of distinguished persons prepared a draft that had only twenty-seven articles. It received the public approval of both the authorities and prominent citizens.

The Constitution recognized Ferdinand VII but stated that no order issued outside Chile could take effect. The king would be a remote symbol, without the power to govern.

The provisional Constitution also provided for a junta and for a Senate, with seven members, and guaranteed the equality of all persons and the freedom of the press.

WAR BREAKS OUT

The viceroy of Peru, Fernando de Abascal, had always mistrusted the criollo movement. When he learned of the bold reforms it had implemented, he decided to crush it by force.

In early 1813 he dispatched Brigadier Antonio Pareja and an expeditionary force, whose numbers were reinforced in Chiloé, Valdivia, and Concepción.

Carrera had to leave the government in order to lead the army on its way south. Several battles forced the viceroy's troops to retreat to Chillán, where they dug in.

The siege of the city, which began in the dead of winter, was a disaster for the Patriots. When Carrera divided his troops, they were attacked at various points by the Royalist forces.

In one of these skirmishes, a surprise night attack, at El Roble, Carrera survived only by throwing himself into the Itata River. Fortunately, Bernardo O'Higgins rallied the soldiers, fought off the enemy, and turned the disaster into a victory.

END OF THE STRUGGLE: RANCAGUA

Because of the poor military leadership, the junta that had succeeded Carrera decided to remove him from his post as commander of the army and to appoint O'Higgins in his stead.

In 1814 a new Royalist expedition, under the command of Brigadier Gabino Gaínza, joined the troops quartered in Chillán.

Disaster of Rancagua.

O'Higgins' first task was to reassemble the Patriots' forces. While doing so, he had to fight the battle of El Quilo; Colonel Juan Mackenna, his able assistant, was attacked at El Membrillar. In both encounters the Royalists were defeated.

O'Higgins was able to intercept Gaínza north of Talca and prevent him from marching on the capital.

When an effort to end the war by means of a treaty failed, a new Spanish leader, Brigadier Mariano Osorio, arrived with reinforcements to continue it.

Carrera had again taken control of the government. Just as a dispute between Carrera and O'Higgins was about to erupt, news of Osorio's expedition led OHiggins to put himself under Carrera's command.

The army hastily prepared to defend the capital. O'Higgins had to quarter his division in Rancagua while awaiting Carrera's arrival. There, he was vigorously attacked by the

Bernardo O'Higgins, the Supreme Director, signed the Proclamation of Independence and the Manifesto to the Nations.

main body of Osorio's troops; no reinforcements arrived. After two days of crushing battle, on October 1 and 2, 1814, O'Higgins and his severely depleted troops made their way to safety at sword point.

The disaster at Rancagua put an end to the period known as *La Patria Vieja*.

The Patriots' leaders and the remnant of the army crossed the cordillera and took refuge in Mendoza, hoping one day to be able to resume the struggle.

The Reconquest

RE-ESTABLISHMENT OF SPANISH RULE

The victory of the Royalists in Chile and throughout Spanish America coincided with the defeat of Napoleon in Europe and the return of Ferdinand VII to the Spanish throne. The king re-established all his powers and governed with extreme harshness; all those in Spain and America who had expressed reformist intentions were persecuted.

Osorio's entry into Santiago meant the repeal of all the measures taken by the Patriots and a return to colonial rule.

Francisco Casimiro Marcó del Pont was appointed governor. One historian describes him as "a cruel, perfumed person" who was ruthless in his actions against the vanquished Patriots.

PERSECUTION OF THE PATRIOTS

Those families who had been in any way involved in the Patriots' cause had to suffer all kinds of abuse and harassment.

The sinister Captain Vicente San Bruno and the regiment of *Talavera de la Reina* were put in charge of maintaining order and surveillance of the citizens.

Some of the most prominent leaders, including innocent old people, were arrested and exiled to the Juan Fernández Islands, where they lived a wretched life.

The possessions of all the Patriots involved were confiscated, and war taxes were also imposed on those who remained in the country.

The repression unleashed by the Spaniards made the king's cause even more unpopular. Chileans who had remained loyal to the Crown or who had been undecided now changed sides to the Patriots. The idea of independence was secretly gaining ground in their hearts.

Juan Fernández Island, from *Gay's Atlas.*

La Cañada, from *Chile Ilustrado* by Tornero.

RESISTANCE

The cause of liberty also began to win over the people. The abuses and arrogance of the Talaveras troops made them hated.

Manuel Rodríguez, a young lawyer who had worked with Carrera, was adept at winning over the people and spreading the Patriots' cause among them. To elude the authorities, who were actively seeking him, he traveled in disguise.

He also used to cross the cordillera to Mendoza, where he and Generals San Martín and O'Higgins coordinated their plans against the Spaniards.

In actions of incredible boldness, Rodríguez and his guerrilla band briefly took control of San Fernando and Melipilla, where they drove out the Royalist authorities and encouraged the people to fight for their country.

La Patria Nueva (The New Fatherland)

THE ARMY OF LIBERATION: CHACABUCO

The Chilean refugees had been welcomed in Mendoza by General José de San Martín, whose intention was to fit out an expedition to liberatè Chile.

O'Higgins and Colonel Ramón Freire organized the Chileans and devoted all their efforts to forming the Army of Liberation, which eventually grew to some 4,800 men.

By early 1817 the expeditionary forces were fully equipped and ready to move out. Small detachments crossed the cordillera in different places in order to mislead the Royalists, while the main force crossed over the Uspallata and Los Patos passes and gathered in the Aconcagua Valley to attack the defenders of Santiago.

The battle took place at Chacabuco, on February 12, 1817.

The Battle of Chacabuco, by Vandorse.

The Battle of Maipú, oil painting by Rugendas.

O'Higgins, heading a division, intrepidly charged against the Royalists and, without any outside help, won a brilliant victory.

Santiago fell to the Patriots, and the Royalists fled to the south and concentrated in Talcahuano.

THE FINAL VICTORY: MAIPÚ

Reinforcements brought from Peru by Brigadier Osorio enabled the Royalists to launch a new offensive against the capital.

At Cancha Rayada, on the outskirts of Talca, the Royalists launched a surprise night attack on San Martín's troops, but thanks to the improvised defense mounted by O'Higgins, some of the Patriots were able to make an orderly retreat.

Desperation spread in Santiago, but Manuel Rodríguez reappeared to rally the people, and under the cry of "We still have a country, citizens!" tried to improvise a defense.

Finally, San Martín was able to reassemble his scattered forces. They fought the Royalists on the fields of Maipú on

April 5, 1818. The Patriots' victory at Maipú was complete and sealed the independence of Chile.

At the end of the battle, O'Higgins, who had been wounded in the arm at Cancha Rayada, joined the battle with some of his men. On meeting San Martín, he congratulated him on his victory.

THE GOVERNMENT OF O'HIGGINS

After the victory of Chacabuco, O'Higgins was elected *Director Supremo* at an assembly of the leading citizens of Santiago.

His government's first concern had been the war against the Royalists. Once victory was achieved, O'Higgins and San Martín devoted themselves to preparing *an expeditionary force to liberate Peru*. The generals knew that the independence of

The First National Fleet, expedition to liberate Peru.

Pine groves of Nahuelbuta, from *Gay's Atlas.*

both the Río de la Plata and Chile would be illusory until a final blow was dealt to the viceroy in Lima.

Despite the overwhelming war debts, O'Higgins and his minister, José Ignacio Zenteno, equipped a powerful flotilla of small vessels that came to be known as the First National Fleet. The fleet was put under the command of the British admiral, Lord Thomas Alexander Cochrane, who, in a daring stroke, captured the forts of Valdivia and later attacked the port of Callao.

In 1820 the army, commanded by San Martín, sailed from Valparaíso, under the protection of the navy, to Peru. The expeditionary force succeeded in landing and capturing Lima, where the independence of Peru was proclaimed.

The chief domestic problems facing O'Higgins included:

a) *War to the death.* The remnant of the Royalist forces defeated at Maipú launched a cruel and devastating campaign in the Biobío region with the support of Indians and outlaws.

Manifiesto de la Independencia 1818

Independence manifesto, 1818.

The Patriots had to fight long and hard to defeat the Royalist leader Vicente Benavides. The execution of Benavides ended the war.

b) *Proclamation of independence.* On February 12, 1818, the independence of Chile was solemnly proclaimed throughout the country. On that day, the final design of the national flag, made by Minister Zenteno, was unveiled.

c) *Republican system.* O'Higgins and his supporters endeavored to establish a solid basis for a republican regime. In that effort, they were opposed by some priests and by Bishop José Santiago Rodríguez Zorrilla, who had to be exiled to Mendoza.

To transform society, the titles of nobility of the aristocracy were abolished. The *Legión del Mérito* was instituted to reward the most outstanding patriots.

Efforts were also made to establish a constitutional system. O'Higgins had been granted full powers, but dissatisfaction surfaced. To quieten it, a constitution was enacted in 1818. It established the authority of the Supreme Director, although it was to some extent checked and balanced by a senate composed of five members chosen by the Director himself.

The Abdication of O'Higgins, oil painting by M.A. Caro.

Valparaíso, 1831.

The constitution also provided for an independent judiciary, with a supreme court at its head.

Nevertheless, neither this constitution nor a second one, promulgated in 1822, fully satisfied the aspirations of the people.

THE ABDICATION OF O'HIGGINS

Mounting discontent marked the five years of O'Higgins' rule, despite the prestige of the Supreme Director.

The influence achieved by the Argentinians and the secret maneuvers of the Logia Lautarina were harshly criticized. The logia was a secret association of politicians and military leaders of the Río de la Plata and Chile. Its purpose was to coordinate the struggle for independence, but its intention were not always clear, and the people were suspicious of its real motives.

The murder of José Manuel Rodríguez in Tiltil and the execution of the Carrera brothers in Mendoza made a sorry impression, and the government came under suspicion.

Moreover, the widespread poverty and the additional taxes imposed to cover the costs of the war fostered further discontent.

The situation became untenable. Called to account by an assembly of prominent citizens, O'Higgins first thought of resisting. But his patriotism and noble spirit prevailed, and he abdicated to prevent bloodshed.

In a passionate speech he asked the assembly to indict and try him for his alleged faults. Instead, he received an ovation and the approbation of his opponents.

After leaving office, O'Higgins went to Peru, where the government awarded him the Hacienda Montalbán in recognition of his efforts on behalf of Peruvian independence. He spent the rest of his life in exile; he died in 1842.

ORGANIZING A NATION
(1823-1861)

Presidents:
Joaquín Prieto, 1831-1841
Manuel Bulnes, 1841-1851
Manuel Montt, 1851-1861

The Organization of Government

CONSEQUENCES OF INDEPENDENCE

The seven years immediately following O'Higgins' departure was a period of relative disorganization due to the war and changes in the republican regime.

The destruction of agriculture and the interruption of trade with Peru, exacerbated by the national effort to maintain the armed forces, especially the expeditionary force to liberate Peru, reduced the nation to unprecedented poverty.

The replacement of the monarchy by a republican government led to the introduction of political changes that, due to inexperience, turned out to be failures. Three more constitutions proved unsuited to the country's needs. There were violent clashes of ideas and a succession of short-lived governments that projected an image of political disorder.

The leadership of the country was in the hands of military officers imbued with liberal ideas, such as Ramón Freire and

Diego Portales.

Francisco Antonio Pinto. Intellectuals such as Juan Egaña and José Miguel Infante were also active in public life.

Despite the difficulties, there was little bloodshed. The statesmen were sincere in their desire to find the best system of government for their country.

FOUNDATIONS OF THE NEW ORGANIZATION OF THE STATE

Ever since independence, efforts had been made to organize Chile according to the liberal ideas of the French Revolution.

Ball at the government palace (detail).

Chile was to be a republic: its rulers were to be elected by the people and were to serve fixed terms of office.

Moreover, the branches of government -the executive, the legislative, and the judicial- were to be separate and independent. The legislative branch or *Congreso* was to be responsible for enacting laws.

In addition, all citizens were to be equal and have the same rights and duties.

Finally, the powers and duties of the branches of government would be regulated by a constitution in order to prevent abuses. This constitution would also stipulate and guarantee the rights of each individual citizen, which the authorities would not be able to violate.

Independence did not produce a change in the social order. The aristocracy maintained its influence and its wealth, and was the only group that could lead the nation.

Both the interests and the feelings of the aristocracy were injured by the disorganization that followed independence. The disorder made business insecure and created a climate of unrest. The reforms implemented by the recent governments clashed with the aristocrats' conservative spirit, and some measures taken against the Church offended their deepest convictions.

But the aristocrats could not remain indifferent to the destiny of the country with which they identified themselves. All they needed was a leader that would make them the government.

DIEGO PORTALES AND HIS POLITICAL BELIEFS

Diego Portales was the scion of an aristocratic family. From early youth he had devoted himself to commerce, with mediocre results. In Peru he had witnessed political anarchy, which had harmed his business. On returning to Chile he observed a similar disorder, and he decided to enter public life.

Political theories were completely irrelevant to Portales. His ideas were incredibly simple. He believed that *order* was an indispensable condition in the life of a nation and that the government was responsible for maintaining order by rigorously applying the law.

Accordingly, what was needed was a *strong executive branch*, with broad authority. The nation's rulers should be *models of virtue*, patriotism, and honesty and inflexible in the performance of their duties.

Portales was not interested in civil liberties or in civil rights, which, in his opinion, always ended in anarchy. How-

José Joaquín Prieto.

ever, he believed that the *authoritarian regime should be provisional*, necessary only until the nation had acquired a civic culture that would enable it to exercise its rights.

Portales' style of governing was "personalistic", and without respect for the law. Interested only in ensuring the authority of the government and its freedom of action, he had little regard for the Constitution of 1833.

PORTALES IN POWER

A political conflict between the liberal groups in power and their oponents prompted an insurrection by General José Joaquín Prieto, commander of the troops in Concepción. Prieto's action was endorsed both by Portales and by a majority of the aristocracy.

The insurrection overthrew the government and placed Vice-President José Tomás Ovalle in command. Armed resis-

Mariano Egaña.

tance by General Freire was unsuccessful: the battle of Lircay (1830) sealed the victory of the new leadership. Portales, appointed to head the government, began to exercise an overwhelming influence. Subsequently, General Prieto was elected president.

In order to secure his power, Portales took rigorous measures. He discharged the army officers and commanders who had defended the government, including Freire. He established the *Guardia Nacional*, a militia composed of citizens of military age, to counterbalance the power of the Army. He persecuted and exiled his most stubborn opponents and silenced the opposition press. He established courts-martial that imposed summary and unappealable sentences on those accused of political offenses.

Despite these measures, a profound unrest pervaded the country, and there were numerous anti-government conspiracies.

THE CONSTITUTION OF 1833

The regime established by Portales and the aristocracy was enshrined in the Constitution of 1833, which regulated the life of the nation for ninety-two years.

The principal architect of the constitution was Mariano Egaña, an eminent jurist, who wrote into it his conservative and authoritarian ideas.

The new constitution granted extraordinary powers to the President of the Republic, whose term of office was limited to two five-year terms.

The responsibilities of the President included the following:

- To participate in the making of laws, jointly with the Congress.
- To issue decrees, regulations, and instructions for the implementation of laws.
- To oversee the proper administration of justice and the professional conduct of judges.
- To appoint and remove ministers, ambassadors, consuls, intendents, and governors.
- To appoint the judges and magistrates of the higher courts.
- To be the head of the armed forces.
- To declare a "state of siege" in one or more areas of the republic in order to enforce extraordinary security measures.
- To use any extraordinary powers that Congress might grant him by means of special laws.

Such powers and duties are usually those of heads of state. But the Constitution of 1833 also granted the president the following attributions, which today appear excessive:

- The President could not be impeached until his term had expired.
- By using his veto power, the President could prevent Congress from passing legislation.
- The President's right of patronage over the Church entitled him to propose to the Pope the ecclesiastics for the higher offices of the Church.
- The municipalities could not take any decisions of importance without the authorization of the governor concerned.

Finally, to ensure that it would endure and be difficult to reform, the constitution stipulated that any amendment required the approval of two successive Congresses, which meant that any attempt at reform would take many years.

The National Destiny

CAUSES OF THE WAR AGAINST THE PERU-BOLIVIA CONFEDERATION

In the 1830's, the existence of Chile as an independent nation was threatened by the Peru-Bolivia Confederation.

Taking advantage of the political chaos in Peru, General Andrés de Santa Cruz, President of Bolivia, invaded the country and obtained the agreement of a segment of the population to form a single nation with Bolivia. Santa Cruz assumed the title of "Protector of the Confederation".

The formation of the Confederation was only a first step for the ambitious Santa Cruz, who dreamed of annexing other

Battle of Yungay (War of the Confederation).

countries to rebuild the old Inca Empire. Chile was one of his targets.

The Chilean government, and in particular Portales, viewed Santa Cruz's plans with concern.

Several issues gradually slid the countries toward war. An old commercial rivalry with Peru, dating back to colonial times, was aggravated by a struggle over customs tariffs. When Peru increased taxes on Chilean products, Chile raised taxes on Peruvian products. A loan granted by Chile during the Peruvian war of independence had not been repaid. Moreover, Santa Cruz was trying to ruin Valparaíso by imposing a special tax on European merchandise stored in that port.

The situation reached a breaking point when Santa Cruz secretly aided the departure of two ships, equipped in Callao, which, under the command of General Ramón Freire, set sail to Chile for the purpose of instigating the country to rebel against President Prieto and Portales.

The attempt failed. In reprisal, Portales ordered two ships to sail for Callao and attack the navy of the Peru-Bolivia Confederation. The surprise action succeeded, and all the rival ships were captured by Chile.

The Chilean government mounted an expedition under the command of Manuel Blanco Encalada. When the preparations were almost finished, Portales traveled to Quillota to inspect part of the troops. Some officers dissatisfied with his policy and, apparently, in collaboration with Santa Cruz, arrested Portales and took him to Valparaíso. The forces quartered in the port resisted the insurgents and held them back near Cerro Barón. In the midst of these events, a lieutenant responsible for guarding Portales ordered him to be shot.

This action horrified the country and further aroused resentment of the Confederation.

The first expedition sent by Chile was a failure. Blanco Encalada, surrounded by superior forces near Arequipa, had to surrender, but was allowed to return to Chile with his men.

Manuel Bulnes.

A second, larger expedition was sent under the command of General Manuel Bulnes.

The Chilean army, which had the support of some Peruvian officers who were dissatisfied with the situation in their country, landed near Lima and took control of the city.

The expedition was called the "Army to restore the freedom of Peru".

Lima's unhealthy climate, and the diseases that decimated General Bulnes' troops, forced him to withdraw to the north, where the provinces had rebelled against Santa Cruz. The Battle of Yungay was fought there, on January 20, 1839.

The defeat of Santa Cruz marked the end of the Peru-Bolivia Confederation.

WAR AND THE NATIONAL SENTIMENT

Although victorious, Chile did not annex any territory, since the only purpose of the war had been to smash the Confederation. By doing so, Chile secured its independence and its military and commercial supremacy in the South American Pacific.

Chile emerged from the conflict considerably strengthened. It had defeated two countries that together were more powerful. The *sense of patriotism* of the Chileans was heightened, and they began to feel great confidence in the destiny of their nation.

The victory of Yungay was regarded as a victory of the Chilean people, symbolized by the *roto* (Chilean common man). To commemorate the event, a plaza and a neighborhood named Yungay were built in Santiago. The "Song of Yungay", with words by Ramón Rengifo and music by José Zapiola, became popular throughout the country.

Since the Conquest, the territory of Chile had extended to the southernmost tip of South America, although that vast region which included Patagonia, the Strait of Magellan, and Tierra del Fuego, was not occupied.

During Manuel Bulnes' administration, there was concern, which had some basis, that a European nation might try to seize the Magellan region. To avert that danger, a fort was built on the Strait.

In 1833 a small schooner, the Ancud, poorly equipped and with scant resources, sailed for the Strait with twenty-one men and two women. The head of the expedition was John Williams, a British captain in the service of Chile.

On the northern border of the Strait, on the Brunswick peninsula, the expedition took possession of the territory and erected some barracks and stockades, which they baptized Fuerte Bulnes. Five years later this settlement was transferred to a more appropriate site, and gave birth to the city of Punta Arenas.

Bases of the Economy

After the wars of independence, the Chilean economy began slowly to revive. Trade, which had been interrupted, was resumed and was reorganized with the growing participation of European agents and commercial firms. Agricultural and mining production increased considerably, and formed the basis of the nation's exports and wealth.

Once Peru gained its independence, Chilean exports of wheat and livestock products to that country were resumed and found a secure market.

Later, Chile began to export these same products to California and then to Australia. The discovery of gold in those regions unleashed a fervor among adventurers who flocked there from all over the world. These newcomers had to be fed. Chile was in a good position to supply these territories, and Chilean farmers promptly responded to the new demand.

More land was cultivated, farm work was intensified, and the construction of irrigation canals and small dams was begun.

As a consequence of this boom, the first efforts were made to introduce modern agricultural implements and semi-mecha-

Manuel Montt, lithograph from the *Galería Nacional*, by Narciso Desmadryl.

117

nized machinery, for example, steel plows and horse-drawn sowing and threshing equipment. Changes were also made in wheat milling, where the first large steam-powered mills were installed to replace water mills.

MINING DEVELOPMENT

Since the end of the colonial period it had been evident that the major wealth of Chile, which was to eclipse agriculture would be mining.

Two metals were paramount in the mining industry: copper, which was beginning to be used on a large scale by European industry, and silver, which was used not only as the local currency but also as the means of payment for imports.

Mining was concentrated in the northern part of the country. Most of the mines were very small and were worked by a large number of small operators, although there were also some large deposits owned by individuals or companies.

The Chañarcillo Mine.

118

Plaza de Copiapó, by R. A. Philippi.

The most important copper mine was the Tamaya, near Ovalle. It was owned by José Tomás Urmeneta, a very enterprising prospector, who had to overcome all kinds of difficulties before discovering the mother lode and successfully exploiting it. The wealth he accumulated allowed him to build a railway from Tamaya to Tongoy, and to establish a large foundry and port facilities there.

The introduction into Chile of the reverberatory furnace, lined internally with special bricks, made it possible to improve the smelting of copper and to better exploit the raw material.

Two of the most important silver mines during the years of independence were Agua Amarga, near Vallenar, and Arqueros, close to La Serena.

But Chañarcillo, south of Copiapó, was the most famous. Discovered by accident by a muleteer, Juan Godoy, it at once attracted a large number of miners, rich and poor, who opened galleries on all sides of the hill.

119

Chañarcillo silver was the source of many large fortunes, and boosted the prosperity of the country. Later, the Tres Puntas deposit and other smaller mines increased silver production even more.

About this time, coal began to be mined on the Arauco coast. The foundries, railways, and steamships stimulated the search for coal.

TRANSPORTATION

During the administrations of Bulnes and Montt, the state and private investors began to modernize the passenger and freight transportation systems.

Better roads, designed and maintained by a corps of engineers, were built in the main regions of the country and permitted the easy movements of carriages where earlier only heavy carts and mule trains could go.

The development of mining in the district of Copiapó led to the construction of the first Chilean railway, which was also one of the first in Latin America. At the initiative of a North American, William Wheelwright, a group of miners pooled resources and financed the project. The railway ran from Copiapó to the port of Caldera, a distance of 80 kilometers. Both the track and the rolling stock were purchased in England.

A little later, Wheelwright began the construction of a railway between Santiago and Valparaíso -a difficult enterprise because of the ranges of hills that had to be crossed.

Steam navigation was also introduced at that time. Together with a group of English investors, Wheelwright founded the Pacific Steam Navigation Company. Two small paddle steamers with port and starboard wheels crossed the Strait of Magellan, and established a shipping line in the South American Pacific Ocean.

Viaduct at Los Maquis; Photograph and Microfilm Archives, Universidad de Chile.

COMMERCE AND BANKING

International trade grew at a rapid pace. Exports, mainly silver, copper, and wheat, financed national development. Manufacturing imports from Europe and the United States ranged from luxury items, such as furniture, china, tableware, and fine fabrics, to tools, coal, and ordinary cloth.

The non-existence of factories in the country meant that Chile was wholly dependent on foreign manufactures.

Several banks were founded in this period, and their lending promoted economic development. These banks were also authorized to issue bank notes, which increased the money supply. These banks financed mining, agriculture, and trade.

The *Caja de Crédito Hipotecario*, established by the government under President Montt for the purpose of granting mortgage loans to farmers, fostered agriculture, although the loan proceeds were not always wisely spent.

Culture

The intellectuals and statesmen of the young republic hoped to raise the nation's cultural level. They despised the culture inherited from the colonial period and wanted to disseminate the most recent European knowledge.

They also thought that great emphasis should be placed on education at all levels. Education would be a way of improving the intellectual and moral standards of the country.

PRESENCE OF FOREIGN INTELLECTUALS. ANDRES BELLO

A number of foreigners with excellent intellectual training arrived in Chile to lend their services and were favorably welcomed by the government of the time.

One of the first to arrive was José Joaquín de Mora, a Spanish man of letters with liberal ideas, who helped to renew the intellectual climate.

In natural sciences and history, Claude Gay warrants special mention. He was hired by the Prieto administration to study the flora and fauna of Chile. After many years of unremitting toil, Gay published his *Historia Física y Política de Chile* in thirty volumes. For

Claude Gay.

the first time, zoology, botany, and the history of Chile were studied with appropiate scientific methods.

Other prominent scientists were the Polish mineralogist Ignacio Domeyko and the Prussian naturalist Rodulfo Amando Philippi.

But the most important intellectual figure was undoubtedly Andrés Bello.

Born in Caracas at the end of the colonial period, Bello distinguished himself from his early youth onward by his pas-

Andrés Bello, by Monvoisin.

sion for study. A long stay in London put him in touch with the European intellectual movement.

Contracted by the Chilean government Bello arrived in the country to fill an administrative position. The facilities he enjoyed and the esteem he was granted by the most cultivated circles enabled him to pursue his activities and acquire an extraordinary fame.

Bello preferred literary studies above all others and was himself a poet of distinction. He expressed his concern for language in many essays and, particularly, in his *Gramática*, a vast treatise in which he put forward an original conception of the Spanish language.

Without having studied law, he became an accomplished jurist. His *Derecho internacional* has been universally praised, and the *Civil Code of the Republic of Chile* was unanimously approved by the National Congress and is one of the best works of its kind. Its provisions were also adopted by several other Latin American countries.

Bello also exercised his influence as an adviser to governments and as a teacher. He published articles on art and literature and commented on many matters of public interest.

The nation expressed its gratitude to Bello by awarding him numerous distinctions and, by means of a special law, granted him Chilean nationality.

In addition to those mentioned, many other intellectuals of lesser renown also left their mark on the nations' culture.

LITERATURE AND PAINTING

Two outstanding aspects of the intellectual movement were literature and painting, which refined the prevailing artistic taste.

José Victorino Lastarria, a young professor at the Instituto Nacional, encouraged a group of his students to cultivate literature. This was the origin of the so-called *Movimiento Literario de 1842*.

Andrés Bello had a deep influence on this movement, especially through his emphasis on the correct use of the Spanish language. Domingo Faustino Sarmiento, an Argentine exile living in Chile, criticized this approach and recommended greater freedom and creative imagination.

The Calle Ahumada in 1834, oil painting by Mauricio Rugendas.

The authors who became most famous were the poet Eusebio Lillo, who wrote the words of the national anthem, and José Joaquín Vallejos, a writer who under the pseudonym Jotabeche, wrote with liveliness and charm of local customs and manners.

In this era, painters discarded the rigidity and *naiveté* of their predecessors and sought perfection of form and naturalness of color.

José Victorino Lastarria.

The French painter, Raymond Monvoisin, who had already made a reputation before arriving in Chile, exerted a marked influence on the artists of his time. His portraits of distinguished members of the aristocracy reveal his sensitivity and perfectionism.

The Bavarian painter, Rugendas, an adventurous and inquiring spirit, became famous for his simple and precise drawings. He was powerfully attracted by simple characters and scenes of daily life. He also sought out exotic and picturesque elements.

Rugendas' landscapes are remarkable for the boldness of his color and the vigor of his brush strokes, which put him ahead of the painters of his era.

DEVELOPMENTS IN EDUCATION

The administrations of Bulnes and Montt both focused their attention on education.

Many new elementary schools were built in cities and towns to teach the three R's and other basic subjects to the poor. The goal was to provide at least a minimum level of education that would help people earn a better living, uplift their moral standards, and enable them to fulfill their civic duties.

The *Escuela Normal de Preceptores* (Teachers Training College) was founded to train teachers and thereby improve elementary education. Another school for women teachers was founded at a later date.

Secondary education was promoted through the creation of *liceos* (secondary schools) in the main cities.

Two technical schools (*Escuela de Agricultura* and *the Escuela de Artes y Oficios*) were also established to provide practical training in productive activities.

However, the most important step was the foundation of the Universidad de Chile in 1843. Its first rector was Andrés Bello.

The new institution, which replaced the old Universidad de San Felipe, received the title of "Protector of Arts, Science and Letters". In its early years it was solely an academic body, responsible for research and dissemination of knowledge. Later it became a teaching institution and professional schools were added.

The university was also responsible for charting the course of, and supervising, the entire national educational system.

EXPANSION
(1861-1891)

Presidents:
José Joaquín Pérez, 1861-1871
Federico Errázuriz Zañartu, 1871-1876
Aníbal Pinto, 1876-1881
Domingo Santa María, 1881-1886
José Manuel Balmaceda, 1886-1891

By the 1860's the nation had established the basis for the rule of law, laid the foundations for economic development, and created conditions for a cultural transformation. It then entered upon a period of accelerated growth and expansion that touched all aspects of national life.

An impressive degree of economic prosperity went hand in hand with greater political liberty and a higher level of cultural development. At the same time, the still unincorporated regions were occupied, and the country expanded to the deserts of the north.

Liberal Politics

The conservative and authoritarian mentality of earlier times
succumbed to the influence of European liberalism.

Politicians and intellectuals -including José Victorino Lastarria, Miguel Luis Amunátegui, and many others- transmitted
and fought for their liberal convictions in books and newspa-
pers as well as in Congress.

The new ideological current sought the greatest political
liberty for the people so that they could act and express their
opinions freely.

José Joaquín Pérez.

Federico Errázuriz Zañartu.

In the economic sphere, the mood was *laissez-faire*: individuals should be free to run their businesses without intervention or regulation by the state. Laissez-faire was also to prevail in international trade; nations were to compete freely; there were to be no trade barriers; and foreign products were not to be burdened with heavy customs duties designed to protect similar domestic products.

VICTORY OF THE LIBERALS

The period of expansion began with the transitional government of José Joaquín Pérez, who sought political peace and used power in a moderate way.

The first liberal president was Federico Errázuriz Zañartu, elected in 1871 with the support of the conservatives, a group he soon shunned. For the next twenty years, all of Chile's presidents were liberals.

Outstanding among them for their character, intelligence, and authoritarianism were Domingo Santa María and José Manuel Balmaceda, who did not hesitate to pursue their policies, even though they encountered harsh criticism and opposition.

CONFLICTS WITH THE CHURCH

According to the liberals, the Church exercised an excessive influence on society and prevented the modernization of ideas and customs. Since the Church was closely connected with the Conservative Party, it was considered a reactionary institution.

To reduce the role of the Church and to ensure freedom of conscience, the liberal statesmen -the most distinguished of whom were Antonio Matta and Domingo Santa María, the future president of the republic- struggled in Congress to deprive the Church of some of its privileges.

The penitent's hood, from *Chile Ilustrado,* by Tornero.

134

Domingo Santa María.

A first step was the enactment of a law that interpreted Article 5 of the Constitution, according to which the official religion of the country was Roman Catholicism, and no other religion could be practiced in public. The new law permitted the practice of any religion, although only in private premises.

A subsequent reform permitted the burial of persons of any faith, not just Roman Catholics, in state cemeteries. This reform provoked a fierce struggle that deeply affected society. The Church forbade its members to bury their dead in state cemeteries, and the government of Domingo Santa María closed Catholic cemeteries. In the end the problem was solved by allowing both kinds of burial grounds to exist.

Civil marriage was also established in the country, separate from the religious sacrament. From then on, the state recognized as valid only those marriages contracted before a civil official.

As a complement to these and other measures, the civil registry was established for the purpose of recording births, marriages, and deaths, which had been previously registered only in parish records.

ELECTORAL FREEDOM

The ability of citizens to freely choose their representatives was one of the basic tenets of liberal thinking.

But it had become customary in Chile for the president of the republic to use his power and influence to openly intervene in the elections. Presidents had persons they trusted elected to Congress, and each president imposed one of his colleagues as the presidential candidate, which ensured his victory.

The struggle over this issue was long and unyielding: it used to flare up before and after each election, and was never satisfactorily solved.

THE GROWING POWER OF CONGRESS

The liberals had their stronghold in Congress, and when liberal candidates won the presidency, their power could not be checked.

Congress was the true forum for discussing and deciding public issues.

By means of several constitutional reforms, the power of the president was reduced while that of Congress was increased.

Among the reforms enacted were:

a) *Presidential term.* Immediately after serving a five-year term, the president could not be re-elected for a second term.

b) *Impeachment of ministers.* The parliamentary procedure for this kind of accusation was simplified.

c) *The Council of State.* A majority of the members of this Council, which advised the president, were to be members of Congress.

d) *Special powers.* Rules were established for the use of special powers by the executive branch during states of siege.

e) *Civil liberties.* The right of unarmed assembly without notice and the right of association were guaranteed.

By means of these and other reforms, Congress increased its importance and began to challenge the executive branch. The great national problems, the governance of the country, and even the actions of public officials were matters of parliamentary concern. Ministers were often summoned before Congress to clarify government policies or to report on specific actions.

The constitution gave Congress some effective powers with which to contest the power of the president: every twelve or eighteen months special laws for approving the national budget, authorizing the collection of taxes, and approving the continued existence of the armed forces had to be enacted.

The need to obtain the enactment of such laws required the government to cooperate with Congress.

Settlement of the Country

Until the middle of the xix th century the activities of the nation had been confined to the area between the Copiapó and Biobío rivers, plus the enclaves of Valdivia, Osorno, Chiloé, and the recently established Fuerte Bulnes.

The general prosperity, the population growth, and the need to increase agricultural production sparked a move to settle regions that had not yet been occupied and a shift of population beyond the then boundary of settlement.

GERMAN SETTLERS

Begun in previous decades, settlement of the lakes region by German immigrants took hold and thrived during the second half of the xix th century.

Molino de San Juan, by R. A. Philippi.

Vicente Pérez Rosales.

Private-sector initiatives and the government's land settlement plan brought some 4,000 German immigrants to Chile in a period of ten years.

This group, albeit relatively small, was able to settle the territories located between Valdivia and the Gulf of Reloncaví.

To oversee the settlement, the government appointed Vicente Pérez Rosales, an indefatigable pioneer who had to

Puerto Montt, twenty years after the arrival of the German settlers.

overcome all kinds of difficulties in the area. He explored the then almost completely unknown region and welcomed the settlers, assigning them land and solving their many problems.

To obtain arable land, the virgin forest had to be burned down and trails hacked through the wilderness.

The German settlers were both enterprising and persevering, and soon reaped the fruits of their efforts. In addition to engaging in agriculture and livestock production, they established small industries for the manufacture of sausages, footwear, beer, furniture, and carriages.

Their prosperity permitted them to found two more cities: Puerto Montt and Puerto Varas.

OCCUPATION OF THE ARAUCANÍA

The peace that reigned along the Biobío River and the relations between the inhabitants on both sides of the frontier made it possible to settle the Araucanía.

Friendly meeting between Cornelio Saavedra and the caciques of the Araucanía.

Some intrepid farmers had already settled in the central valley, south of the Biobío River, by buying, leasing, or simply taking the land from the Indians. On the coast, the existence of Fort Arauco and coal mining afforded another line of penetration.

During the presidency of José Joaquín Pérez, the government took steps to incorporate the Araucanía. This enterprise was carried out by Colonel Cornelio Saavedra, who within a short time occupied the territories as far as the Malleco River and refounded the city of Angol. On the coast he advanced as far as the Toltén River.

This first initiative was achieved almost without bloodshed, until the Indians who lived near the Malleco River and were led by the cacique Quilapán, staged an uprising. After the

Mining camp at Caracoles.

defeat of the Indians, settlement was halted for a few years, but by the time the War of the Pacific broke out, settlement had resumed and reached the Traiguén River.

During the conflict with Peru and Bolivia, fewer Chilean soldiers were stationed in the Araucanía, and the Indians took advantage of this circumstance to attack the frontier posts.

After the Lima campaign, which all but brought the war to an end, the occupation could be resumed. The troops advanced up to the Cautín River, and the city of Temuco was founded in 1881.

Colonel Gregorio Urrutia was in charge of the occupation of the remaining territory. He built several forts and pushed on to Lake Villarrica, where he refounded the city of Villarrica.

The task begun by the Spaniards 300 years earlier had come to an end.

PIONEERS IN THE NORTHERN DESERTS

The remarkable mineral wealth in the deserts of the north was an abiding incentive for many adventurers and businessmen. They undertook hazardous expeditions to explore the hills,

142

pampas, and ravines. Some were in search of silver; others hoped to find copper, guano, or nitrate.

One of the earliest pioneers was the Chango López, a modest man who discovered guano in Mejillones. After incessant explorations, he finally settled in the Caleta de Antofagasta, which was uninhabited at the time. This was the origin of the settlement that was later to become a city.

Another enterprising explorer was José Santos Ossa, who financed and headed several expeditions. On one of them he discovered saltpeter in the Salar del Carmen, in the hinterland of Antofagasta. His discovery made him a very wealthy man.

The discovery of the famous silver mine of Caracoles, near Calama, attracted large numbers of miners and laid the basis for activities in the region.

All these ventures were taking place in territory claimed by Bolivia, which in one way or another asserted its sovereignty there.

However, the workers, technical experts, businessmen, and capital were all Chilean. In addition, food and mining equipment were supplied from Valparaíso. It was in that port that arrangements for the export of minerals from the north were made.

Bolivian sovereignty was purely theoretical.

International Conflicts

THE WAR WITH SPAIN AND THE AMERICANIST SENTIMENT

During the 1860's, Spain tried to enforce claims on some of its former colonies: it seized Santo Domingo and, in a joint action with England and France, it put pressure on Mexico for the payment of its debts.

When France invaded Mexico and tried to impose Maximilian of Austria as emperor, a pitiless war began.

Such acts by the European powers awoke feelings of indignation and solidarity among the Latin American countries. Concurrently, Spain made claims on Peru for the repayment of debts and other matters. Two Spanish warships sailed to Peru to support these claims.

With unwonted speed, the Spanish forces seized the Chincha Islands, whose guano deposits were the wealth of Peru.

This action unleashed a fateful chain of events. Chile stood by Peru and, by declaring coal to be a war contraband, prevented the Spanish fleet, which had been strengthened by other powerful ships, from being bunkered.

The head of the Spanish fleet, José Manuel Pareja, ordered a blockade of Chilean ports. This strategy proved unsuccessful and ended disastrously for Pareja. Juan Williams Rebolledo, commander of the corvette *Esmeralda*, one of the two ships Chile possessed, surprised the Spanish schooner *Covadonga* and forced it to surrender in the naval battle of *Papudo*. Pareja could not endure his defeat and committed suicide.

The new Spanish chief, Casto Méndez Núñez, pursued the Chilean and Peruvian ships, which had sought refuge in the channels of the Chiloé region, but he could not destroy them. He fruitlessly attacked them at Abtao, but did not dare to come too close for fear of the reefs that protected the allied ships.

The war continued to no purpose and to the detriment of Spanish prestige. This situation led the Spanish government to order an increase in hostilities.

On March 31, 1866, Méndez Núñez ordered the bombardment of Valparaíso. The port had no defenses so the Spanish ships acted mercilessly.

For three hours the city, which had been abandoned by its inhabitants, came under enemy fire. The attack focused on public buildings, customs warehouses, and port facilities. The damage was enormous.

The ill-starred Spanish venture ended with an attack on the port of Callao, whose fortresses strongly repelled the offensive.

Chile's solidarity with Peru had a high cost. Other Latin American countries did not follow its lead, and before long a conspiracy of its neighbors placed Chile in difficult straits.

BACKGROUND OF THE PACIFIC WAR

The Spanish Crown had never concerned itself with establishing precise borders for each colony. This lack of clearly defined borders was the cause of many disputes between neighboring countries.

Since the colonial era, the northern border of Chile had been the Atacama Desert, an imprecise expression that lent

Aníbal Pinto, President of Chile at the outbreak of the Pacific War.

Arturo Prat Chacón.

itself to various interpretations. The Chilean government asserted that the border should be fixed at the 23rd parallel -that is, as far north as Mejillones- but Bolivia argued that the border was at the 25th parallel -the southern border of its sovereignty.

Several rounds of negotiations failed to resolve the issue. However, a treaty signed in 1873 established the border at the 24th parallel and contained a commitment by Bolivia not to raise taxes on Chilean companies operating between the 23rd and 24th parallels.

In the same year, Peru signed a secret treaty with Bolivia pledging mutual support in the event of war. It also sought an alliance with Argentina, which was about to sign the treaty.

Peru's primary motive for these plans was the difficulties of its nitrate industry in Tarapacá. The Peruvian government had nationalized the nitrate mines in order to obtain more revenues for the state. By allying itself with Bolivia it could better compete with Chile in nitrate mining.

Five years after the secret treaty was signed, the Bolivian dictator's Hilarión Daza, ordered a tax to be levied on the nitrate exports of the Compañía de Salitres de Antofagasta. When the company refused to pay the tax, Daza ordered its property to be auctioned off.

On the day of the auction, several Chilean warships landed troops at Antofagasta and occupied the city. They were warmly welcomed by the population, almost all of which was Chilean.

THE PACIFIC WAR

Antofagasta was occupied in February 1879. For the next four years, the conflict continued in a series of campaigns.

Chile's primary concern was to secure control of the sea. The naval forces were more or less equal: Peru had the armored ships *Huáscar* and *Independencia*, and Chile the *Cochrane* and the *Blanco*. Both belligerents also had some steam-powered wooden frigates and corvettes.

The Chilean fleet, under the command of Juan Williams Rebolledo, was unsuccessful in its pursuit of enemy vessels. However, during an expedition to Callao, Chile secured its first moral and material victory at Iquique.

The *Esmeralda* and the *Covadonga*, under the command of Arturo Prat and Carlos Condell, were surprised by the *Huáscar* and the *Independencia*, which were superior in armor, artillery, and speed.

Prat gave the order to face them nonetheless, but his fragile vessel could not resist for long. Miguel Grau, commander of the

147

Sinking of the Esmeralda.

Huáscar, decided to put a quick end to the attack by ramming the *Esmeralda* with his formidable armored ship. This maneuver was used by Prat and some of his men to make a desperate effort to board the enemy ship; all of them died in the attempt.

The *Esmeralda* sank, though its crew kept firing until the end.

In the meantime the *Covadonga* had sailed south, pursued by the *Independencia*. Condell steered his ship extremely skillfully, navigating very close to the shore, where he hoped the Peruvian vessel, with deeper draft, would run aground. His plan was successful: The *Independencia* foundered on some submerged rocks, capsized, and sank.

Chile had lost an old and ill-equipped vessel; Peru had lost its most powerful ship.

But the most important fact was the heroism of Prat and his crew, whose moral example was to lead the Chilean forces to final victory.

Later, the *Huáscar*, under Grau's skillful command, attacked several Chilean ships and ports, creating considerable

Battle of Chorrillos, by Juan Mochi.

Manuel Baquedano.

disruption, until he was surprised by Chilean armored vessels at Angamos. The *Huáscar* was forced to surrender after a battle in which its brave commander met his death.

From then on, with the three armored ships it possessed, Chile exercised an almost total control of the sea.

Once control of the sea had been secured, the invasion of Peru could begin. The Tarapacá campaign made it possible to exercise control over that region and to exploit the rich nitrate deposits there; next, the provinces of Tacna and Arica were captured; and, finally, an expeditionary force of 20,000 men landed south of Lima. The battles of Chorrillo and Miraflores opened the gates of the Peruvian capital.

It was still necessary to wage a difficult campaign in the Peruvian Andes, where some soldiers and guerrilla forces were operating under the command of intrepid leaders.

In one of the battles, at La Concepción, a Chilean company of seventy-seven soldiers was annihilated.

END OF THE WAR

In 1883 a provisional government established in Peru put an end to the conflict by signing the *Treaty of Ancón* with Chile.

Peru permanently ceded to Chile the territory of *Tarapacá* and temporarily ceded *Tacna* and *Arica*. The final status of those two territories was to be decided in 1893 by a plebiscite (This plebiscite was never held, but in 1929 an agreement was reached whereby Peru recovered Tacna, and Chile retained Arica.).

As for Bolivia, a simple truce declared the end of the war. While this pact was in force, Chile was to continue to occupy the territory of Antofagasta. When the treaty was finally signed in 1904, Bolivia ceded the territory of Antofagasta, and Chile pledged to build a railway from Arica to La Paz, to allow the free transit of Bolivian merchandise, and to pay a cash compensation.

The battle of Concepción.

For Chile, the War of the Pacific meant a considerable increase in its territory and the acquisition of priceless nitrate and copper deposits. Thereafter economic prosperity increased and public and private wealth made it possible to undertake a large number of important development projects.

FRONTIER PROBLEMS WITH ARGENTINA

The kings of Spain had granted the governors of Chile a vast jurisdiction that included the territory of Patagonia on the other side of the cordillera and extended without limits to the south. However, in practice it was not possible to occupy those regions.

During the republican period, the only attempts to incorporate a portion of these territories was the construction of

Fuerte Bulnes and the founding of Punta Arenas. Thanks to these initiatives, Chile was able to assert its rights to the Strait of Magellan.

In the mid-nineteenth century a border dispute with Argentina began. The lengthy negotiations were unsuccessful, and in Chile the idea that Patagonia was of no value began to prevail. Furthermore, there were no ties whatsoever with that region and no possibility of settling it.

The eyes of the country were fixed solely on the north, which held out the promise of great mineral wealth.

During the Pacific War, while Chilean forces were advancing in the deserts, beyond the Andes Argentine forces were gradually moving through Patagonia. After the war, and in the middle of a threatening international situation, a frontier treaty was signed with the government of Buenos Aires in 1881. This treaty stipulated that the frontier was to run along the *highest summits of the cordillera*. Thus, in one stroke, Chile renounced all the territory located on the other side of the mountains.

In exchange, the treaty gave Chile full dominion over the Strait of Magellan. Tierra del Fuego, divided by a north-south line, would be Chilean on the west and Argentine on the east.

After the treaty was signed, the border had to be accurately fixed. This delimitation necessitated extremely lengthy discussions between a Chilean and an Argentine expert of those points at which the relief was not clear. Diego Barros Arana, the Chilean expert, worked unceasingly, studying all the information available to him.

The points on which the experts failed to reach an agreement, principally in the southern region, were submitted to the British Crown for arbitration. In 1902 an award was issued that tried to satisfy both parties, although it did not fully respect the reasons adduced by either country.

The arbitration did not definitely resolve the issue: new disputes and interpretations of the award have continued to give rise to problems.

Economic Prosperity

The growth of the Latin American and European population and the need to feed it spurred the development of agriculture in Chile.

Earlier, exports had been exclusively to countries on the Pacific seaboard, but now the Atlantic markets were open as well. Wheat, for example, was exported to Argentina, Brazil, and Great Britain.

The increase in agricultural production was due to the incorporation of the Araucanía and to the German land settlement. Other contributing factors were improvements in agricultural techniques and the introduction of new plant and animal species.

Irrigation canals, some of great length, were built by private farmers, who were thus able to bring more land under cultivation. The use of fertilizers, although insufficient, and the import of steam-powered machinery and new implements helped boost production.

Among the new agricultural plants, French vines, brought by the owners of large vineyards, were the most noteworthy. Since then Chilean wine has been of outstanding quality and has been awarded prizes at international fairs.

Livestock was upgraded through the introduction of breeding animals that made it possible to renew the national herd. Dutch cattle, good producers of milk and beef, were a great success. In the Magellan region, the introduction of merino sheep -which were raised for both wool and meat- was a major factor in regional development.

The spectacular development of industrialism in Europe and the United States demanded an ever greater supply of raw materials. Countries that had mineral resources, as did Chile, responded to this demand by increasing production.

Copper, whose production in Chile had been growing for several decades, became a major export. Chile became the largest copper producer in the world, and taxes on cooper financed half the national budget for a number of years.

There was also a boom in silver mining. The Caracoles mine produced far more than Chañarcillo, and although the former was located in Bolivian territory, it primarily benefited the Chilean economy.

Nitrate plant.

Crushers at a nitrate plant, drawing by Melton Prior.

Coal from the Schwager and Lota mines captured the domestic market and began to be exported to other Latin American countries.

However, it was *nitrate* that gave an unprecedented boost to the country's economy.

Well before the Pacific War, Chilean entrepreneurs and workers had participated in nitrate mining in Peru and Bolivia. After the conflict, when the nitrate provinces passed into Chilean hands, the country held the world monopoly of nitrate.

But only a small part of the ownership of the nitrate was in Chilean hands. More than half of the plants were owned by British companies, as were the nitrate railways. Thus a considerable part of this wealth benefited foreign investors.

Copper mine at El Teniente.

The increasing American and European demand for fertilizers with which to improve agricultural production, gave a decisive impetus to nitrate mining. Shipments of this product were the most important Chilean export.

As the following figures show, nitrate production rose rapidly:

Year	Tonnage
1878	350,000
1900	1,470,000

Export taxes on nitrate considerably augmented government revenue and made it possible to pay off the debts incurred during the Pacific War and to undertake an ambitious public works program.

President Balmaceda's administration demonstrated a notable concern for executing public works. In Balmaceda's view, the wealth from nitrate would be short-lived and should be invested in permanent projects while it lasted.

Communications were improved and considerably expanded. New first-class highways with good bridges were built and the railways penetrated remote regions. Several branches from the main north-south line pierced the Araucanía, boldly

*Construction of the Malleco Viaduct,
inaugurated in 1890 by President Balmaceda.*

A session of Balmaceda's cabinet.

crossing rugged terrain. The most significant project, both in conception and in achievement, was the *Malleco Viaduct*, designed by the Chilean engineer Aurelio Lastarria.

Seawalls and piers were built in the ports, and a dry dock was constructed in Talcahuano.

Large buildings for educational institutions, hospitals, and government offices sprang up in cities across the country.

Water supply services and street paving were expanded in the main cities. In Santiago the Mapocho River was finally channeled by the construction of secure embankments.

The Revolution of 1891

During Balmaceda's presidential term, the ongoing power struggle between the Congress and the executive branch came to a head.

The president was a strong, proud man, and he zealously guarded his authority. But his plans and policies were repeatedly obstructed by constant battles with party groups in Congress. On several occasions he was forced to replace his ministers.

The opposition criticized the President's public works program, which they considered to be extravagant and they would not forgive him for his authoritarianism. The situation worsened when the rumor spread that the President intended to impose one of his colleagues as his successor.

The President, for his part, would not accept the predominance of Congress and insisted that the full powers of the executive be maintained.

By late 1890, the political situation had become extremely tense. Balmaceda knew that Congress would not approve the budget for the coming year if he did not appoint a cabinet acceptable to a majority of the representatives. He therefore decided to promulgate the same budget as in the previous year. In doing so, the President violated the constitution.

Congress responded by deposing the head of state.

ESCALATION OF THE CONFLICT

Congress' position was supported by the navy, which set sail to the north from Valparaíso.

José Manuel Balmaceda

A *government junta* was established in Iquique; its main task was to organize an army. To that end it relied on the miners from the desert and the funds provided by nitrate. On Balmaceda's side was the army of the central and southern regions.

The conflict had to be resolved by arms. The pro-Congress troops sailed in transport ships under the escort of the navy and landed in Quinteros. They attacked and defeated the government detachments at Concón and forced their way across the Aconcagua River. Days later, they had to fight a new battle at Placilla, on the outskirts of Valparaíso. The forces of Balmaceda, defeated at Concón, had received reinforcements and were able to establish a defensive line. But the pro-Congress troops defeated them once more, in what proved to be the final battle of the war.

Upon hearing of this defeat, Balmaceda secretly took refuge in the Argentine embassy and committed suicide on the very day on which his mandate ended.

THE CRISIS OF LIBERAL SOCIETY
(1891-1920)

Presidents:
Jorge Montt, 1891-1896
Federico Errázuriz Echaurren, 1896-1901
Germán Riesco, 1901-1906
Pedro Montt, 1906-1910
Ramón Barros Luco, 1910-1915
Juan Luis Sanfuentes, 1915-1920

The victory of Congress in 1891 implied the establishment of a parliamentary regime in which the authority of the president was substantially reduced. Congress now began to play a paramount role in public affairs and impose cabinets to its liking on the president.

To effect this shift in the balance of power, no amendments to the constitution were needed; it was simply a matter of interpreting it in accordance with Congress' point of view.

The political situation created by the upper classes represented in Congress, fulfilled their ideals of liberty. But severe economic and social problems that were left unsolved eventually brought about the collapse of the system.

Economy and Society

INFLATION AND THE NITRATE CRISIS

Ever since the establishment of private banks, which were authorized to issue currency, inflation had been a national problem: the value of the currency declined, and the prices of products rose.

Later the state began to issue its own currency, which further fueled inflation.

In addition, the economy was buffeted by a sharp decline in the export of nitrate, which could not compete with the less expensive synthetic nitrate produced in Europe. After World War I (1914-1918), the synthetic nitrate industry became well established and the production of natural nitrate in Chile plummeted. This situation marked the onset of the so-called nitrate crisis, which intensified even more in the 1930's.

THE AWAKENING OF THE LABOR MOVEMENT

The presence of masses of workers in the main cities, ports, and mining centers gave birth to the first labor organizations. Initially they were only mutual aid associations; then some trade unions, and finally national organizations that represented vast sectors of the workforce.

Concurrently, labor leaders and the labor press indoctrinated workers in how to fight for their rights.

POVERTY AND UNREST

The living conditions of the ordinary people were wretched. In the cities, they crowded into unhealthy tenements, where vice,

Santiago, circa 1900: Horse-drawn carriages in front of the main campus of the Universidad de Chile.

filth, and disease prevailed. In the mining camps, housing consisted of zinc or wooden shacks that offered little protection against the elements.

Work was dangerous, and there was no provision for workers who suffered an accident or fell ill.

Wages did not keep pace with inflation, and because of their high price clothing and food were pitiable.

Because of these conditions, unrest grew and spread among workers, and the nation's worsening economic problems added fuel to the flame.

During the first decade of the century, there were strikes in Valparaíso, Santiago, and Iquique. They ended tragically, with many deaths and considerable property damage.

The economic development of the xix th century, the expansion of the state, and the spread of public education produced a growing middle class.

Commercial establishments, stores, and small factories provided jobs for the lower middle class and enabled them to improve their economic status. The public administration was manned by government workers who through length of service could work their way up. Likewise, in the army career officers could move through the ranks, and come to hold positions of relative importance.

The remarkable development of public education at all levels also helped to improve the cultural status of the middle class.

Secondary schools that offered young people intellectual and moral training, prepared them for entrance to the universities or for office work in the public and private sectors. The university educated the professionals, who constituted the upper middle class; their education and prestige enabled them to exert influence in public life.

In the first decades of the xx th century, the middle class was already an important sector of society, and felt called upon to participate in the leadership of the nation.

The Political Framework

THE PREDOMINANCE OF CONGRESS

By reducing the authority of the executive branch, the parliamentary system made the president a more or less decorative figure. No longer could he set the course of the nation.

Since the president's ministers had to have legislative support, they were obliged to shape their policies to the opinions of the congressional majority; otherwise, the Congress approved a vote of no confidence and forced the cabinet to resign.

This power of the Congress was the source of a constant political struggle between the executive branch and Congress, and among the parliamentary groups that allied or divided themselves at their convenience. The result was deplorable: the continual fall of cabinets, called *ministerial rotation*, impaired government action and the nation's problems, instead of being solved, only grew worse.

THE "SOCIAL QUESTION"

The "social question" was the term used at the time to refer to the problems of the workers and the unrest that prevailed among them.

Despite the strikes and the struggle of the unions to obtain a minimum standard of living and the prevention of industrial accidents, the upper class that governed the country tried to ignore the seriousness of the situation.

Only the Church, some writers, and some people of good will spoke out on these problems and made isolated attempts to find a solution. But these efforts were insufficient.

Also ineffectual were the activities of the newly formed Democratic Party and the change in policy of the Radical Party, which consisted mainly of middle-class people who embraced the ideal of social change.

Nonetheless, the situation had come to a head and a profound political upheaval was imminent.

RECENT HISTORY
(1920-1973)

Presidents:

Arturo Alessandri, 1920-1925
Emiliano Figueroa, 1925-1927
Carlos Ibáñez, 1927-1931
Juan Esteban Montero, 1931-1932
Arturo Alessandri, 1932-1938
Pedro Aguirre Cerda, 1938-1941
Juan Antonio Ríos, 1941-1946
Gabriel González Videla, 1946-1952
Carlos Ibáñez, 1952-1958
Jorge Alessandri, 1958-1964
Eduardo Frei, 1964-1970
Salvador Allende, 1970-1973

The crisis of the liberal oligarchic regime made it possible for the middle and working classes to exert their influence, which was reflected in political and social reforms. Efforts were also made to accelerate economic development through state intervention in the economy. The major successes of this policy were achieved in energy production and industrialization.

Democratization led to a strengthening of the unions, better living standards and welfare, housing, health, and public education programs. The expansion of education was notable, as was the flowering of arts and literature.

The Political Movement
of 1920

ARTURO ALESSANDRI AND HIS PROGRAM

Alessandri was a politician of great intelligence and a brilliant orator who knew how to win over the masses. He showed his metal as a courageous leader during a senatorial election in Tarapacá, when he won a hard-fought victory over a Conserva-

Arturo Alessandri Palma.

tive rival. Thereafter, he was nicknamed "The Lion of Tarapacá".

Alessandri's special sensibility allowed him to understand the nation's social problem and design a plan of reforms. According to his philosophy, a government could avoid revolution by opening the way to evolution. If this were done, the necessary changes could be peacefully made.

After being named a candidate for president by an alliance of the Liberal, Radical and Democratic parties, Alessandri drafted a very daring reform program. First, the presidential system of government had to be reestablished so as to ensure that the head of state could really direct the course of the nation.

Next, the problems of the working class had to be solved by means of labor legislation that would guarantee the rights of workers. Special courts would settle disputes between labor and management.

In the economic area, Alessandri proposed the stabilizing of the currency to prevent its devaluation, and a tax reform that included the establishment of an income tax whereby wealthier citizens would pay higher taxes.

Other proposals in his program were respect for electoral freedom, equal justice for women, universal and compulsory elementary education, and the separation of Church and state.

His program was enthusiastically supported by the middle class and powerfully attracted the working class, who viewed it as the realization of its hopes.

SUCCESSES AND DIFFICULTIES IN GOVERNMENT

The elections of 1920, although won by a narrow margin, were a major victory over the old aristocracy and the upper classes of society.

However, the hopes awakened by Alessandri's victory were soon dispelled. The opposition of the Senate prevented the president from solving the nation's major problems, so that by the end of four years, no progress had been made.

Congress continued to obstruct the executive branch.

The difficult economic situation was to produce a political crisis. While the country was expecting Congress to enact a law allocating funds with which to pay government workers and servicemen, whose pay had decreased because of devaluation, the Senate and the Chamber of Deputies approved a law on *parliamentary emoluments* to cover the expenses of senators and deputies.

Arturo Gordon.

Claudio Matte and Darío Salas, educators of the early XX century.

This action fueled the discontent of the population at large and of young army officers.

THE MILITARY MOVEMENT OF 1924 OPENS THE WAY TO SOCIAL REFORMS

Reacting to Congress' vote to approve parliamentary emoluments, a group of army officers went to the galleries of the Senate where they "rattled their sabers". This demonstration showed how serious the situation had become, and confirmed the rumor that a military movement was afoot.

The military exerted pressure on Congress and tended to support the President in his battle to implement social and political reforms.

Thanks to the efforts of the President and to the pressure brought to bear by the military, Congress immediately enacted several social laws.

The reform package included legislation on labor contracts, organization of unions, mediation and arbitration tribunals, industrial accidents, workmen's compensation insurance, and a private sector employees retirement plan.

The promulgation of the social reform laws was a landmark in Chilean history. For the first time, Congress had decisively framed a comprehensive policy in favor of blue-collar and white collar workers. Ever since, wage earners have been protected in their relations with employers and companies, insured against occupational accidents and diseases, and guaranteed the right to retire.

These laws, which were supplemented in subsequent years, placed Chile in the forefront of social legislation in the Americas.

After the social reform laws had been enacted, Alessandri, feeling supplanted by the military, offered his resignation, but Congress, instead of accepting it, granted him permission to leave the country. Alessandri then left for Europe.

THE CONSTITUTION OF 1925

A military junta and a civilian junta succeeded each other in government. The latter, representing the mainstream of public opinion, asked Alessandri to return to Chile, resume his presidency, and re-establish the normal institutional framework.

Alessandri returned in triumph and devoted himself to preparing the constitutional reforms that the nation wanted for putting an end to the parliamentary regime.

An advisory commission composed of representatives of the political parties and various institutions, prepared draft constitutional reforms that were later ratified by plebiscite.

The main provisions were:

a)   The power of Congress periodically to enact laws to authorize the collection of taxes and to maintain the armed forces was eliminated. Instead, the laws on these matters would be permanent.

b)   A time limit was placed on the annual debate by Congress of the budget law.

c) The presidential term of office was lengthened from five years to six.

d)   The oversight of election procedures, which had been the responsibility of the Senate and the Chamber of Deputies, was assigned to an independent body, the *Tribunal Calificador de Elecciones*.

e)   The separation of Church and state was guaranteed, which put an end to the old disputes between believers and nonbelievers.

f)   One of the more remarkable provisions, indicative of the new spirit, was a pledge that the state would guarantee "the protection of labor, industry, and social security programs, especially those for adequate housing and living conditions, so as to ensure every citizen a minimum level of wellbeing, sufficient to satisfy his personal needs and those of his family".

The state would also favor the division of property and the constitution of family property.

g)   Proprietary rights, which had previously been unrestricted, were now subject to rules commensurate with the progress of society.

In reality, the constitutional reform of 1925 was equivalent to the creation of a new legal code -new in its inspiration and implications- for the life of the nation. The independence of the executive and the legislative branches was clearly defined, and since then the president has had broad powers for governing the country.

The promulgation of the Constitution of 1925 did not put an end to the nation's political problems, which reflected social and ideological conflicts. The intervention of the military in politics also helped to disturb the stability of the country.

In 1927 Colonel Carlos Ibáñez brought about the fall of President Emiliano Figueroa. Ibáñez was then elected President and, for a time, governed according to the law. But he soon became a dictator who violated the law and persecuted his opponents. Finally, in the wake of a general strike of all sectors of society, Ibáñez had to leave office.

The political instability continued. A rebellion had to be quelled by the Air Force and the Army. In 1932 Ibáñez's democratically elected successor, Juan Esteban Montero, who represented the civilian reaction against the military, was

Carlos Ibáñez del Campo.

overthrown by the Air Force and infantry regiments. A junta of socialist inspiration replaced him, until one of its members, Carlos Dávila, took control and dispensed with his colleagues. Dávila's "one hundred days" were very productive in initiatives, but chaos and uncertainty prevailed, and he, too, had to leave office. The aspirations for a civilian government and the need for order prevailed, however, and even the military understood that legitimacy had to be restored.

In 1932 Arturo Alessandri was again elected president. He was faced with the tasks of consolidating the constitutional regime and taking economic measures to rehabilitate public finances. He succeeded in pulling the country out of the severe depression brought about by the economic crisis of 1929 and the political crises of 1931 and 1932.

Democratic Reformism

A new era was ushered in by the election of Pedro Aguirre Cerda to the presidency in 1938. A candidate of the *Frente Popular*, a coalition of parties of the left and the center, he was the first president to come from the Radical Party.

Aguirre Cerda's victory signified popular endorsement of a social policy that would improve the situation of the less fortunate sectors of society. The concern for workers and employees strengthened the unions and their national organizations.

Aguirre Cerda, and the presidents who followed him, emphasized economic development above all else. To this end, state-owned enterprises backed by considerable capital and financed by foreign loans were established. The state thus became an active participant in the nation's economic life, because private companies on their own had been unable to develop the economy.

President Juan Antonio Ríos.

Aguirre Cerda was succeeded by Juan Antonio Ríos and Gabriel González Videla, both of whom continued his policies and were able to achieve considerable progress in social and economic development.

They, in turn, were succeeded by Carlos Ibáñez and Jorge Alessandri, who had different ideological positions. Next came President Eduardo Frei Montalva of the Christian Democratic Party, who, influenced by the Church's social doctrine, tried to incorporate the neediest sectors of society into the economic and social life of the nation.

The victory of the political forces of the left, Marxist in inspiration, gave the presidency to Salvador Allende in 1970 and swept the country towards policies aimed at establishing Marxist socialism. The government, however, could not control the extremist groups that supported it and chaotic situations occurred. The economy rapidly deteriorated, social harmony was disrupted, and the institutional framework was seriously threatened.

By September 1973 the situation was very confused. The opposition, both in Congress and in the press, was vigorously voicing its objections. The majority of the citizens were expressing discontent and some trade associations, including the truck

The nitrate crisis.

179

owners and the copper workers trade union, were openly challenging the authorities. In these circumstances, the armed forces decided to intervene. The military violently overthrew Allende's government, which was replaced by a junta led by General Augusto Pinochet.

In Pursuit of Economic Development

THE NITRATE CRISIS

The spectacular boom in nitrate mining, and the wealth it gave the country, began to fade in the second decade of this century.

World demand for nitrate had reached a level that could hardly be surpassed. Several nations were trying to find a substitute and were experimenting with the manufacture of artificial nitrate.

The First World War (19141918) was decisive for the decline of the nitrate industry: Germany, isolated by the war, was forced to step up the manufacture of synthetic nitrate, and after the war other nations did the same.

From then on exports of Chilean nitrate began to decline, as did prices on the world market.

During Alessandri's first administration, the situation in the nitrate mining industry became dramatic. The companies that mined the deposits had to curtail their operations, and a number of plants were shut down.

A large number of workers were dismissed, and the widespread unemployment posed a serious labor problem.

With the drop in nitrate exports, state revenues from export taxes declined.

The magnitude of the crisis was unprecedented. The great wealth derived from nitrate was decreasing, and with it the economic prosperity that had favored the affluent classes.

A second crisis, more severe than the first, hit the country in 1929 and lasted many years. This crisis was the result of the Great Depression, which originated in Europe and the United States and affected the entire world.

Nitrate mining was again the sector that suffered the most, but all economic activities were hard hit.

Unemployment in the nitrate region reached catastrophic levels, and large groups of unemployed workers had to be transferred to the center of the country. The state had to feed this mass of unemployed each day.

Santiago.

The crisis was so severe that its effects persisted for many years. The economic situation of the country was difficult to improve: The price of Chile's export products, such as nitrate, fell sharply. This decline meant that the country had less money with which to buy the industrial imports it needed, such as machinery, vehicles, tools, and foods that were not produced domestically.

THE RECOVERY IN COPPER MINING

The copper mining industry, which had been important in the past, began to revive in the early years of this century.

The growing demand for copper for industrial use all over the world induced some American companies to prospect for copper deposits in Chile. This search led to the opening of the El Teniente, Potrerillos, and Chuquicamata copper mines, of which the last-mentioned was the most important.

The new mines required large capital investments and were equipped with the most modern machinery.

Copper came to replace nitrate as Chile's main export, and export taxes on copper became the largest source of revenue for the state.

MODERNIZATION: TRANSPORTATION AND THE CITIES

Great changes occurred during the first half of this century in both passenger and freight transportation.

This modernization was based on improved coal and steam technologies, but the most important changes were due to the use of electricity and petroleum.

New machines such as electric and diesel locomotives, automobiles, trucks and airplanes revolutionized transportation. Load capacity and speeds improved.

Aerial view of Santiago in 1925.

The appearence of cities also changed considerably. One of the most important causes was the use of cement in buildings, houses, and pavements. The use of electricity expanded, while the telephone and radio broadcasting made communications easier.

Horse-drawn carriages and streetcars ceased to be used for urban transport and were replaced by electrical streetcars, buses, and automobiles.

Water supply and sewerage systems were constructed and improved the quality of life of the population.

FOUNDATION OF ECONOMIC DEVELOPMENT

After the nitrate crisis and the depression of 1929, successive governments tried to solve the nation's economic problems.

Under President Pedro Aguirre Cerda, long-range development plans to be implemented by the state were carefully drafted by well-trained professionals and technical experts.

183

Only vigorous action by the state, which had the necessary capital and organizational capacity at its disposal, could transform the country's economy.

A technical body, the Corporación de Fomento de la Producción (CORFO), was entrusted with the planning and implementation of the various projects. The following activities were the result of its efforts:

a) An electrification plan designed to overcome the deficit in electricity production was studied. To this end, the Empresa Nacional de Electricidad (ENDESA) was established, and in the course of time the shortfall was eliminated.

Numerous hydroelectric and some thermoelectric power plants were built throughout the country, and were connected to form a national power grid.

Thanks to excellent planning, which took future consumption into account, Chile has had sufficient electricity for industrial development ever since.

b) An adequate supply of fuel was a serious problem, since it had to be imported at a high price.

CORFO promoted oil prospecting in Tierra del Fuego. It was unsuccessful for some years, but in 1945 the valuable fuel was found in the Magellan region.

A specialized agency, the Empresa Nacional de Petróleo (ENAP), was established to develop the field. As a result, the production of oil, oil derivatives, and liquid gas increased. ENAP later built refineries to process various oil by-products.

Domestic fuel production has been insufficient to cover the needs of transportation and industry, so the country has to continue to import oil. Nevertheless, domestic oil production has been a very important factor in economic development.

c) Industrialization required the establishment of a domestic steel industry. Iron ore deposits in the La Serena region and coal in the province of Arauco provided the raw materials for this endeavor.

To implement this project the Compañía de Acero del Pacífico (CAP) was established. It constructed a huge steel plant at Huachipato, on the San Vicente Bay, near Concepción.

The production of steel was a significant development and enabled many industries to begin to manufacture modern products.

d) Copper mining also received some attention in the new plans. To help small and medium producers, the Paipote foundry, belonging to the Empresa Nacional de Minería (ENAMI), was built near Copiapó.

In addition to these measures, CORFO undertook other, less important, activities. It also supported the establishment of new private-sector industries by providing them with technical assistance and acting as guarantor of credits obtained abroad.

Accordingly, state action was fundamental in transforming the economy in the middle of this century.

Later on, other important economic measures were taken. The large copper mines were nationalized, the state holding the majority interest in each company. In addition, expansion and modernization plans were agreed upon and increased production considerably. Subsequently, the state expropriated the shares that had remained in private hands, and became the sole owner of the companies. A specialized agency, CODELCO, took control of the mining companies and the marketing of copper.

To spur agricultural production, a broad agrarian reform program was implemented, albeit with considerable difficulty. The production of some crops such as sugar beet was stepped up, and sugar production became the responsibility of a state agency, IANSA. Agricultural credit and technical assistance was also improved.

Under state sponsorship and a protectionist policy, a number of private-sector industries were developed such as those for engineering products, home appliances, pulp and paper, plastics, automobile assembly and fisheries.

The nation's economic development was reflected in public works, highways, airports, ports, and housing and in higher wages and a better standard of living for wage earners.

Social Change

THE MIDDLE CLASS

The new conditions in the country were mirrored in particular by the more visible presence in society of the middle and the working classes.

The middle class, which was already a prominent sector, exercised strong influence and power. It was favored by the expansion of the state's functions and the social orientation of politics. It formed part of a profuse decision-making bureaucracy that promoted the new social and economic policy and respected democracy and the law.

The standard of living of the middle class improved considerably and upward social mobility made it one of the largest sectors of society.

THE WORKING CLASS: URBAN AND RURAL

Economic development in manufacturing, mining, industry, and construction was responsible for increasing the working class, improving its standard of living, and uniting it in its trade union and political struggles.

The trade unions succeeded in obtaining some advantages for their members, particularly in wages, although these would rapidly deteriorate because of inflation. The right to strike was the expedient used by workers to obtain benefits.

Trade unions in the same economic sector formed confederations, and organizations like the CTCH and CUT (Central Unica de Trabajadores) were successful for a time in unifying the entire labor movement.

There were no radical changes in the life of rural workers, although the cities influenced them to some extent, modifying their customs and fostering the use of new material goods. Towards the end of this period, authorization to form trade unions affected the less remote regions, and the agrarian reform attempted to redistribute land ownership and improve the life of rural workers.

OTHER SOCIAL CHANGES

The growth of cities has been phenomenal, Santiago has sprawled and the Valparaíso-Viña del Mar conurbation and Concepción have spread almost as quickly.

This change has been due to the expansion of industry, commerce, and the administration, as well as the attraction of life in the city. The city fascinates the rural dweller and this attraction creates a new problem: The lack of jobs produces widespread poverty and marginalization. Shantytowns, which are a serious social problem, spring up on the outskirts of the large cities.

Despite a vigorous public housing policy, which has resulted in the large-scale construction of housing for workers and employees, it has not yet been possible to solve this persistent problem.

Another major change has been the role of women, not only in the home but also in employment and in public life. The spread of education and the need to increase the family income have been the determining factors.

The increasing empowerment of women has enabled them to acquire political rights, in which area they have exercised a moderating influence.

The substantial development of the nation's public education system in the xix th century and the coming of age of its culture paved the way for the achievements of the xx th century.

The extension of elementary education through the construction of many public schools and compulsory school attendance (mandated in 1920) have raised the level of general education, even though many poor children do not attend school.

Gabriela Mistral.

Pablo Neruda.

Secondary education has also been extended through public secondary schools and a number of private colleges.

In higher education, the Universidad de Chile has modernized and broadened its activities and emphasizes research in the humanities (e.g., history, literature, and linguistics) and in the natural sciences. The contribution of other universities, including the Universidad Católica de Chile, the Universidad de Concepción, and the Universidad Técnica del Estado (now the Universidad de Santiago), has been mainly in education.

Within the realm of intellectual activities, the social sciences, particularly economics and sociology, have been added

189

to the humanities. But the field of outstanding achievement has certainly been that of literature and the arts.

In poetry, Gabriela Mistral and Pablo Neruda, both of whom were awarded the Nobel Prize for Literature, have attained worldwide prestige. Neruda has been the more successful. His many works, full of felicious expressions and evocative imagery, have been published in countless editions and translated into many languages.

In the novel, the most significant authors are Mariano Latorre and Eduardo Barrios, both of whom wrote about Chilean customs and manners, but many other writers have enjoyed literary success.

As a result of the cultural extension services of the Universidad de Chile -and, later, of those of other universities- music and the theater attained high standards. The university's experimental theater troupe has staged the most important classical and modern plays. The university's symphony orchestra, choir, and ballet have presented excellent concerts and performances featuring accomplished Chilean and international artists.

THE NATION CHANGES COURSE

Presidents:

Salvador Allende, 1970-1973
Augusto Pinochet, 1973-1990
Patricio Aylwin, 1990-1994
Eduardo Frei Ruiz-Tagle, 1994-

During the second half of the xxth century the world was sharply divided into two camps: on the one hand, the democracies, represented by the United States, the countries of Western Europe, and Latin America; on the other, the communist bloc, which comprised the Soviet Union, China, and their satellites in Eastern Europe and Asia. These two blocs waged a "cold war" or struggle to exert influence and pressure to impose their ideologies. In our hemisphere, Cuba, whose revolution was led by Fidel Castro, entered the Soviet orbit and endeavored to spread the communist revolution to other countries.

Chile did not escape the influence of these events, which stirred up the left-wing parties and spurred the revolutionary groups to violence.

Around 1990 the communist countries entered a period of crisis, brought about by the failure of their economic and social plans and abuse of power by their dictatorial goverments. The countries of Eastern Europe broke away from the Soviet system, and the Soviet Union fell to pieces; out of them arose a number of states that turned towards democracy.

Jorge Alessandri Rodríguez.

These events ended the antagonism between democracy and comunism that had marked the course of the century.

HOSTILITY AND VIOLENCE

Buoyed up by the hope of a forthcoming revolution, the Communist and Socialist Parties had gradually infiltrated the life of the nation, while extremists groups, such as the MIR, were promoting violent revolution. Fear and disorder pervaded the country.

In 1970 the left-wing forces elected Salvador Allende president by a narrow margin, and swept the country towards policies aimed at imposing socialism. The government, with the cautious support of the Communist Party, endeavored to

Eduardo Frei M. and Salvador Allende.

mantain an image of respect for law and traditional institutions, but could not restrain the socialists and the extremists groups that supported it; chaos ensued. The economy quickly succumbed, the social compact crumbled, and the legal system was seriously impaired.

By September 1973, havoc reigned. The opposition took a hard line both in the National Congress and in the press. Most citizens voiced their discontent, and some trade associations

Havoc reigned.

193

and trade unions, for example the Truckers Association and the Copper Miners Trade Union, openly defied the established authorities.

In these circumstances, the Armed Forces decided to intervene and, with a violent coup d'état, overthrew the goverment. Allende committed suicide in La Moneda when he realized that resistance was useless.

La Moneda burns.

A governing junta took command. It was headed by General Augusto Pinochet, who soon asserted his authority over his colleagues and assumed the title of President of the Republic. The military dictatorship lasted far more than sixteen years.

General Augusto Pinochet.

Its first task was to consolidate the regime being put in place. Left-wing forces were vigorously persecuted, imprisoned, tortured and sent into exile. About 3000 were executed. The secret services of the Armed Forces and of the Uniformed Police, such as the DINA, acted without restraint.

The violation of human rights provoked reactions throughout the world, and Chile was ostracised by the international community.

The labor movement and the trade unions were held in check while the large national and foreign companies were favored.

The different branches of the Armed Forces held different positions. While the Army and the Navy were hard-liners, the Air Force disagreed with the personalism of Pinochet and the

FIRST PUBLIC PROTEST

Our primary concern is the climate of insecurity and fear, whose roots, we believe, lie in accusations, false rumors, and lack of participation and of information.

Also of concern to us are the social aspects of the present economic situation, including the increase in unemployment and the arbitrary or ideologically motivated dismissals. We fear that, with a view to promoting economic development, the economy is being organized in such a way that wage earners are called upon to bear an excessive burden of sacrifice, without having a desirable degree of participation in this reorganization.

We are also disturbed by the fact that the educational system is being comprehensively restructured and directed, without parents and the school community having sufficient participation in these efforts.

Our final concern is that, in some cases, there is a lack of effective legal safeguards for personal security. This lack results in arbitrary or excessively prolonged detentions; during them, neither the persons concerned nor their family members can ascertain the specific grounds for such detentions. It also leads to interrogations in which physical and moral duress is used; to limitations on the possibilities of legal aid; to sentences for the same crime that differ in length in different areas; and to restrictions on the normal use of the right to appeal.

(Pastoral Letter of the Catholic Church dated 24 April 1984)

The "No" campaign against Pinochet.

more repressive measures taken. Its Commander-in-Chief, General Gustavo Leigh, was forced to resign. The Uniformed Police took a complacent stance and obtained a number of benefits.

A constitution was framed by the goverment and approved by a plebiscite in 1980. While it embodied some modern aspects of public life, through various means it ensured the future influence of the Armed Forces and of the right-wing parties identified with them.

THE TRANSITION

Discontent with the military goverment grew apace and, despite the difficulties it encountered, the opposition was able to voice its criticisms. Finally, the military goverment called an election.

The winner by a good margin was Patricio Aylwin, a member of the Christian Democracy Party, who coupled his

Patricio Aylwin.

long political experience with the ability required in difficult circumstances.

Aylwin took office in 1990 and governed for four years. His main task was to pave the way for a transition and to promote harmony among all sectors of society. In this endeavor he was fully successful. Relations with other countries returned to normal, and Chile regained its standing in the community of nations.

The efforts of his goverment were hampered by the continuation in office of General Pinochet as Commander-in-Chief of the Army, while his supporters in the National Congress prevented justice from being done for the violation of human rights and blocked a reform of the Constitution that would have permitted the establishment of a really democratic society.

In the economic sphere, public works, construction and exports were strongly expanded. In 1994, Aylwin was succeeded by Eduardo Frei Ruiz-Tagle, who was also elected by a wide margin. His goverment aspired to overcome the antagonism with the Armed Forces by adopting a complaisant attitude towards them. The thrust of President Frei's goverment was progress in education, public health, and infrastructure as an

Eduardo Frei Ruiz-Tagle.

essential factor in economic development and the accompanying social progress.

Restructuring of the Economy

REVOLUTIONARY ECONOMICS

The earlier doctrine of a state-controlled economy and of the role of large state corporations that had managed to promote development and raise the standard of living was distorted by the goverment of President Allende to the point of exaggeration. Adopting demagogic policies it raised wages and salaries, which triggered rampant inflation; people had money, but prices kept rising and all goods, including essential foodstuffs, disappeared from the market.

Action to introduce an agrarian reform was stepped up; the large, foreign-owned copper-mining companies were nationalized and no compensation was paid. The banking industry was taken over by the goverment. Legal loopholes and take-overs by workers were used as grounds for expropiating large and small factories.

Chaos and uncertainty were all pervasive.

RESURGENCE OF FREE ENTERPRISE

The economic doctrine of free enterprise, which was thought to have been buried some seventy years before, reappeared, and was strengthened under the goverment of General Pinochet. The military goverment had no economic doctrine of its own but embraced that put forward by the so-called Chicago Boys, a group of economists who had been trained at the University

National investments increase.

of Chicago and advocated the most orthodox form of capitalism. It was intended to promote the interests of businessmen and private enterprise and, in this way, to increase national and foreign investments. This policy would benefit the upper classes of society and some day, perhaps, the poor as well, at least so it was thought.

The goverment paid the foreign corporations for the mines that had been expropriated, and encouraged the investment of foreign capital in new mining operations. It returned the banks to their former owners, and took over their debt, which it repaid with public funds. It also gave back to their owners the factories that had been taken over and the farms that had been expropriated as part of the agrarian reform. Various state-owned enterprises were sold cheaply to powerful economic groups. It pursued a policy of privatization.

It transferred social security, medical care, and pension services to private enterprises, namely the ISAPRES and the AFP's.

Public outlays for the Armed Forces were increased, while those for education and health were reduced, the last-mentioned alarmingly so. At the outset little attention was paid to public works and housing.

Before this economic policy began to show results, the middle-and low-income sectors were hard hit. Widespread unemployment depressed the standard of living, and violence and crime reached unprecedented levels.

Towards the end of the 1990's the economic model began to show positive results; during the goverments of Aylwin and Frei-Ruiz Tagle the macroeconomic variables were kept in balance and the economy took off.

National and foreign investments continued to be promoted, exports rose, inflation fell, and the value of the currency was kept stable.

The national budget was restructured to permit larger capital and current outlays on education, health, and public works. Wages and salaries increased somewhat in real terms.

The private sector, benefitting from the economic policy pursued, demonstrated unexpected managerial ability and dynamism. Companies devoted to mining, pulp and paper-making, fruit-growing, electricity and telecommunications

Privatization increased.

Santiago stock exchange.

flourished. In this new economic climate they increased both their capital and their earnings.

The upper classes of society were those that benefitted most from this new wealth. Sales of luxury and sumptuary goods soared. The availability of expensive products led to a buying spree, from which not even the lower middle class was immune. In the midst of this boom, pockets of absolute poverty still remained.

EDUCATION AND CULTURE

Political activism in the universities and secondary schools, in which left-wing and center-right students took the leading parts, dated back many years. The military goverment took control of the universities, reduced the budgets of the University of Chile and of the State Technical University, and harassed

203

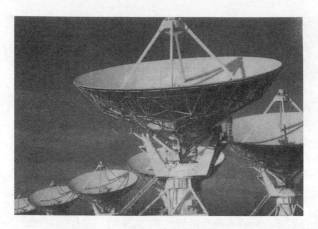

Chile regained its standing in the community of nations.

those who disagreed with its ideology. At the same time it authorized the establishment of institutes of higher learning and private universities belonging to economic groups and to groups intellectually akin to it. The intellectual standing and facilities of most of these institutions were inadequate. The work of intellectuals and performers was monitored and what was called a cultural blackout occurred.

When the democratic goverments came back into office, the universities regained their independence. Thanks to the spontaneous efforts of writers and performers, and the financial support of those goverments, a "cultural spring" ensued. The National Library and public libraries throughout the country, impaired by lack of funds, began to buy books again.